To Dawn, Agape and the big-G.
—DANA TESONE

*To Carol—life-long friend, listener,
and confidant.*
—PETER RICCI

Contents

PART 4 *Hospitality Operations Cases*

Preface

This book is a collection of stories extracted from practicing managers in the hospitality industry. For the purposes of this book, the hospitality industry is defined as lodging, food service, theme parks, attractions, resorts, recreation, events, transportation, and entertainment venues. The managers who tell their stories have worked within these industry sectors, as well as in myriad functional specializations of management including operations, marketing, sales, security, human resources, finance, and administration. They range from top-level executives to middle- and junior-level department managers. The authors have narrowed and crafted these experiences into the case studies presented in this *Little Book*.

Suggestions for the Reader

The book consists of forty-five case studies, arranged within four parts. The *Micro Cases* in Part One of the book focus on single-issue management strategies aimed at problem solving and performance enhancement in hospitality organizations. Part Two contains *Case Vignettes* that address practical (applied) skills for managers and supervisors to use on the job. Part Three presents the reader with *Case Vignettes in Human Resource Management* to reinforce applications of people-management skills in all areas of hospitality management. Part Four of the book contains cases in *Hospitality Operations* that may be considered from any functional viewpoint of management.

    The intention of each case is to highlight a set of circumstances that require management decision-making practices in any type of operation. Many of the cases take place in lodging facilities including medium- to large-scale hotels and resorts. A number of cases take place within various dining room environments including hotel food and beverage outlets, catering facilities, and freestanding independent and chain restaurants. Other settings include theme parks, an events management firm, a convention center, a vacation ownership property, transportation functions, cruise lines, and casino/hotels.

Questions are presented within each case to guide readers in the application of knowledge in hospitality management to scenarios that exist in the real world. It is recommended that the reader reflect on actual scenarios in the workplace or try classroom role-playing while reading this book. It is recommended that college departments and corporate training programs use this *Little Book* as an ancillary resource across the hospitality curriculum. The cases are designed to foster new awareness on the part of the reader within the context of each course or workshop in a college or corporate training curriculum.

A Note to Educators and Trainers

The book is written in an easy-to-read style for both practitioners and students. The authors possess more than forty years of experience as practitioners at all levels of hospitality management. If the printed questions are used in the classroom, educators may choose to expand them. For practitioners, the printed questions are similar to those asked by many involved in these actual events.

The book is written at a level intended for all audiences, from those in advanced tourism magnet programs in high schools to seasoned practitioners who are currently working in the operations field and want to analyze different ways to handle scenarios. The cases have all been tested in classroom environments.

Acknowledgements

The authors would like to give special thanks to the following reviewers:
George Alexakis, Nova Southeastern University
Kim Susbauer, Cuyahoga Community College
Faye Jackson, The University of Houston

How to Analyze a Case

Most upper-level courses involve written or oral case studies presented for analysis. There is a method to be employed when analyzing a case study. The purpose of the case study is to demonstrate the ability to apply concepts learned through class activities to practical scenarios in business and industry. This concept is called *synthesis*. Synthesis is the demonstrated ability to apply abstract concepts in a practical setting for the purpose of making decisions that lead to problem solution or proactive organizational practice.

Steps in Analyzing a Case Study:

1. Review the facts of the case study. A case study will vary in length from a few paragraphs to many pages of information. The information presented identifies a scenario that calls for analysis. The first step is to carefully read the case study for the purpose of extracting important facts. Not all facts are relevant. The reader determines relevancy of the facts based on the nature of the case study.
2. Some case studies list questions at the end of the case. Others do not. If questions are listed, they should be read after the first reading of the case study. A second reading of the case study will verify those facts originally deemed to be relevant to the purpose of the case.
3. Review the collection of facts in their relationship to each other. The purpose of this step is to identify patterns that may emerge when the facts of the case are reviewed in their entirety. A pattern will reveal the overriding purpose of the case study. For instance, a collection of facts may point toward organization design and structure issues. Thus, the overall purpose of the case is to conduct an analysis of facts to determine recommendations for organization design.
4. Based on your review of the facts, determine the major issues for consideration. In most cases there will be numerous issues. In this

step, the reader identifies symptoms that lead to problems or opportunities for enhanced productivity.

5. After analyzing each major issue, identify at least three alternative actions for problem solving or improved productivity. Analyze each alternative for feasibility. Determine which of the alternatives is most viable. The optimum alternative may be cost prohibitive so that the reader would not be likely to recommend it, even though it would have the best outcome.

6. Based on recommended alternatives, suggest a sequenced course of action. Identify who does what, when, where, and how in this section. Include how the action plan would be evaluated. Conclude with projected outcomes associated with the action plan.

PART 1
Micro Cases in Management Strategies

CASE 1
Productivity
Enhancement

Note: There are many available models to describe organizational productivity. At the most basic level, all models include three sections: inputs (resource allocation), transformational process (conversion), and outputs (products/services).

You are a supervisor in the transportation department of a major theme park. The department director has called all the managers and supervisors together for a brainstorming session on how to enhance productivity. Some people recommend slashing costs as the answer, while others suggest revenue increases only. Still others focus on streamlining transformation processes as the sole answer.

After hours of discussion, the director steps up to address your group. She says, "Guys, productivity is a balancing act." She draws the productivity model on a flip chart. "You can't focus on the left side without addressing the right side of the model. You have to consider both sides when enhancing productivity, which means if you take action on the right side, you must take action on the left side." She continues, "For right now, let's forget about the middle. That will come in handy when we decide how to fix both the left and right sides of our model." She concludes, "As I see it, there are only three ways to do this, although if you are really creative, there may be a fourth one that will work."

Question: What are the three or four things?

Hint: The solution has something to do with increases, decreases, and maintaining levels on each side of the model.

CASE 2
Leading a Turnaround Strategy

You have just been hired as a supervisor for a security department at a large resort. You notice that the staff appears to be lax, with many of them failing to meet standards for performance. During your assessment of the work unit you learn that former supervisors were somewhat apathetic and failed to exercise solid supervisory techniques such as communicating standards for performance and training new staff. Now you have inherited a group of individuals who are unfamiliar with the standards and have never been trained. While you really can't blame them for their substandard performance, you must turn this work unit around. This will require firmly communicated and enforced standards for performance and retraining of the existing staff.

Questions: What will be your leadership style during this intervention? Will you act as a transactional leader or a transformational leader?

Hint: Is it too soon to use one of these, given the nature of this situation?

CASE 3
Value-Added Restaurant Service

You work as a floor manager in an upscale dining room on the dinner shift. On one particular evening you observe a server who is able to provide superlative service to your guests, who are mostly great tippers. At the end of the evening the server cashes out and learns that he has made over $500 in gratuities. Instead of being greedy, he decides to tip the busser $100, and he gives the bartender and the captain $50 each. Then he walks back to the dish room and gives each dishwashing attendant $5, for a total of $25. His net gratuities for the evening are now down to $275.

Questions: How might he benefit from being so generous with his gratuities? What kind of help do you think he will get on the next shift?

Hints:
1. The busser makes the server's job easier and provides him with table turnovers.
2. The captain influences the maitre d' when it comes to seating and does wine and flambé service at the tables.
3. There never seems to be enough clean china, glass, and silverware for the server to provide service to the guests.

CASE 4
Training Strategies

You are a food and beverage supervisor for a large resort hotel. You have just been transferred from one of the dining rooms to one of the cocktail lounges. The beverage manager tells you that there have been numerous complaints about how long it takes to get drink orders and check totals. He tells you to set up a training program to fix the problem.

You start working in the lounge and find that there is only one point-of-sale (POS) terminal for servers to ring in orders and total checks. As far as you can tell, the servers seem to comply with the standards for service and are frustrated while waiting in line to enter their orders. You set up a meeting with the beverage manager.

You tell him that you have conducted a needs analysis and there is no learning gap, and thus no training problem. You explain that there is a resource problem (POS hardware shortage) and a systems problem (a breakdown in order placement). He replies that a new system has been ordered, and additional terminals will be installed next week. He assures you that the single pre-check terminal will be replaced with three machines as part of the new system.

Questions: Do you have a training situation at this point? How will you proceed with the training?

Hint: This would be a skills training project.

CASE 5
Turnaround Strategies and Employee Relations

You are a human resources practitioner for an events management firm. You know that one of the departments has been poorly run for about two years. The manager of that department has recently been replaced with an individual who is charged with turning the unit into a productive working area. You have been warned that such an intervention will create negative "ripples" among some of the existing staff members, who are accustomed to engaging in unproductive behaviors. It is the intention of the new manager to "weed out" certain poor performers.

Sure enough, the employees are starting to run to you with complaints and grievances about how the new manager is treating them.

Question: How do you handle these?

Hint: Refusing to listen to them is not an option.

CASE 6
Rules and Progressive Discipline

You are a front office manager at a medium-size branded hotel. The hotel follows corporate SOPs to the letter. Your best front desk agent was notified last week that he has been selected by the corporation for the Manager in Training (MIT) program upon his graduation from school this semester. This news has him and you quite motivated, as he really wants a management career with this chain.

One night it is extremely busy at the front desk, with long check-in lines. Your star agent has picked up his bank from the general cashier, placed it into the terminal drawer, and started checking in guests. Some of the other agents see the crowd before they pick up their banks, and jump behind the desk to help with check-ins. Contrary to company policy, your star agent lets other agents use his bank. At the close of the shift, he is exactly $200 short. According to company policy, any bank discrepancy over a certain amount is grounds for disciplinary action. Also, an individual who has a disciplinary notice in his or her personnel file is ineligible to participate in the MIT program. He offers to replace the money from his own pocket. But company policy prohibits that, and even if he did it, the disciplinary action would still be required. You know that one of his coworkers ripped him off, but you can't prove it. It was also his fault because company policy prohibits giving other individuals access to a personal bank. You feel sympathy for this guy because this incident will ruin his opportunity to break into management.

Question: What are you going to do?

Hint: There are rules and there are exceptions to rules, but exceptions include risk.

CASE 7
A New Management Assignment

You are a supervisor for a small work unit consisting of five workers. The previous two supervisors were fired for poor performance. Needless to say, the workers are doubtful about whether you will be any more successful than your predecessors. It is interesting that the work group has bonded in a way as a result of poor leadership, and is pretty self-sufficient when it comes to doing the job. You know that the first thing you must do is earn their respect. Once this is done, you will want to build a team.

Question: How will you earn their respect and then build a team?

Hint: Setting a good example and demonstrating stewardship could help with both objectives.

CASE 8
Dealing with Problem Employees

You are hired as a manager for a department that is in need of improvement. You assess the situation by walking around and conducting individual discussions with each employee. You find that there is a general feeling of apathy among all the staff members. Usually, you find some workers whom you can turn around, but you are beginning to believe that this will not be the case with anyone on this crew. You are starting to come to the conclusion that you may have to "clean house" in this department. You consider doing a mass hiring to replace every position.

You go down to the human resources office and review the files of your crew members. To your surprise, you find that they have all been rated at levels of above average to excellent over the past three years!

Question: Now what do you do?

Hint: You must be fair, uniform, and consistent in your management practices.

PART 2
Case Vignettes in Management and Supervision

CASE 9
The Restaurant

You are a manager for an upscale restaurant. As you make your rounds on the dining room floor on a Tuesday night, you observe a server who is tableside. Dante, the server, has a party of three—a dad, a mom, and their little six-year-old daughter. After serving the drink order, he approaches the table to take the orders for appetizers and entrees. The little girl interrupts him and says, "Sir, my birthday is in two days and I would like a special treat. I was wondering if you have my favorite flavor of ice cream, butter pecan." Dante smiles at her and says, "Well, we don't have that flavor, but I'll tell you what. While you are eating your dinner, I'll go in the back and make you some. I know how to make the best butter pecan ice cream you ever had. Would you like that?"

Needless to say, the little girl is ecstatic. Dante takes the orders, returns to the kitchen, and hands a dishwashing attendant $10. He tells him, "Run across to the convenience store and buy me a pint of butter pecan ice cream . . . and by the way, keep the change."

Preliminary Questions:
1. Why is Dante telling lies to the guests?
2. What do you think about him sending the dishwashing attendant to the convenience store?
3. Would you address this issue with Dante? What would you say to him?

More about the Case: As the family is finishing their entrees, Dante begins to prepare his "special" dessert for the little girl. He scoops the ice cream into a footed parfait bowl, adds toasted almond sprinkles delicately over the scoop, and tops it with a generous fresh whipped-cream cap, complete with a maraschino cherry placed on top of his masterpiece. Dante places the parfait bowl on a doily-lined four-inch plate along with a demitasse spoon so his little guest may savor each dab of the ice cream treat. Next, he finds the biggest chocolate-dipped strawberry available and places it strategically on the liner (this is mom's treat, since she is too diet-conscious to order her own dessert).

As the entree plates are cleared, Dante asks the little girl if she is ready for the special ice cream treat. After all, he says, "I have been slaving away in the back to make your special blend." He presents the plate and asks the girl if she might want to give her strawberry to mommy.

While the little girl indulges in the best-tasting ice cream she ever ate and mom partakes in her oversized berry, Dante punches in $12 on the "open food" key, which adds nicely to the check total. Meanwhile, mom reminds dad to treat Dante very well when he pays the bill.

More Questions:
1. Describe the experience that Dante has created in the minds of the little girl, her mother, and her father.
2. Do you think they will share this experience with their friends? How do you think they will describe it?
3. Do you think Dante learned this kind of service in a training program, or is he just naturally creative?

Conclusion: At the end of the evening, when the restaurant is closed and all the sidework is completed, you as the manager may want to have an informal chat with Dante. You could tell him to follow company policy and to provide only those items that are on the menu. You could also tell him to avoid disturbing the dishwashing attendant, and to come to you when he wants to do something special.

Or you could have a conversation that is similar to the following:

"Dante, you have just created 'magic' for this family of three. You profiled the group and noticed that the key was to make the mom happy. You chose to do this by doing some magic for her little girl's request. The little girl is happy, mom is happy (which makes dad happy), your sales total on the check is $12 higher (which makes the restaurant happy), and your 30 percent gratuity is calculated on that total, which should make you happy. And don't forget the dishwashing attendant, who is happy with the $6 change he received from his trip across the courtyard."

"This is the service imperative, or 'magic,' as those of us in hospitality like to call it. You have created a memorable experience for a few people, with very little effort on your part. This is what makes you a 'value-added worker.' Tomorrow, we must share this technique with the rest of the staff. After all, if we provided this type of experience for all of our guests, we would be the hottest expensive restaurant in town."

But, of course, you are the manager, so how you choose to handle this situation is up to you.

CASE 10
Career Paths

You work at a large resort and are taking a coffee break in the employee cafeteria. The director of human resources sits down with you. His name is Danny and he is about twenty years older than you. After some chitchat, you ask him how he got to where he is in his career. He sits back, gazes upward, and starts to tell his story.

"I came from a lower-middle-class, broken family," he begins. "When I was sixteen, I started working at a local hotel just to earn some extra money, and by the time I was seventeen I was working full time. My goal was to get out of the house by the time I was eighteen, which I did. I took college courses, but was more interested in making money. By the time I was twenty, I had worked in just about every hotel job there was. Then I was promoted to management and learned how to work with people as a supervisor through the trial-and-error method, which was not always fun. However, I was lucky enough to have plenty of mentors who showed me how to be a better manager. I was really ambitious back then, and got promoted to the next level of management every two years or so. I really worked hard and found that I enjoyed turning operations around and developing other workers."

Preliminary Questions:

1. Are there workers in hospitality who enjoy successful careers without ever finishing college? Give a specific example of someone you know or someone you heard about who fits this profile.
2. Do you think most large hospitality companies require college degrees for executive administrative positions like accounting,

human resources, and marketing? Why would a company require this level of training, in your opinion?

Conclusion: Danny continues, "But then I got really burned out on operations management. I noticed that the human resources director seemed to have better working hours than the ops managers and spent most of her time helping the employees. Although I had lots of college credits, I didn't have a degree, which was a requirement for the job. So, I went back to school to get my degree in my off-hours. Between school and work, I was really learning a lot about management at that time. Finally, after a few years, I got my degree and a job as the number-two manager in the human resources department. By now I was working on my master's degree on weekends; I was eventually promoted to human resources director."

"But don't you want to be a GM?" you ask. He says, "I thought I did back then, but when they offered me those promotions, I turned them down. You see, I am at a stage where I really love the work I do, even though I could make more money by going back into operations. I like helping people, and in this position I have the time to focus on other aspects of my personal development. I'm on a different journey these days than I was back in my achievement years. But I'll tell you this: I am a lot happier with my life than most of my friends."

The next thing you know, time has flown by and it's time to go back to work. As you do, you keep Danny's story in the back of your mind.

Conclusion Questions:
1. Would you consider Danny to have been lucky, ambitious, or both?
2. What can you take with you from this story?

CASE 11
A Comparison of Management Styles

You work as a security officer at a large resort. Because of your classes at the university, you work an overlapping shift between the day and early night shifts. There is a security manager who supervises each shift. You work four hours with the alpha shift manager (Brad) and four hours with the beta shift manager (Sharon). Both managers are former police officers and are very proficient in safety and security procedures. The difference between these two individuals as managers, however, is like day and night (no pun intended).

Brad is a micromanager who doesn't believe in employee empowerment. He commonly casts blame on the officers for their mistakes, but he is the first to take credit for the ideas of others. He is a stickler for policies and procedures, even when it seems there should be exceptions based on a set of circumstances. He tends to have favorites on his shift who receive preferential treatment over some of the other, harder-working officers. The officers don't complain about Brad to the director because Brad seems intimidating. Brad often berates the officers in front of their peers and the guests.

Preliminary Questions:
1. Are you or someone you know familiar with this type of manager?
2. Provide a specific example of just such a manager, without naming that person.

Conclusion: Sharon, on the other hand, is every bit as proficient as Brad in the technical aspects of security, but she is also respected as a leader among the officers on her shift. As a matter of fact, most of the officers in the department request transfers to her shift when there are open positions. She is considered to be firm but fair in her approach with the officers. She often takes the blame for things that go wrong, even if it was caused by one of her officers. She always listens to the staff for new ideas to improve performance and takes action to implement good ideas. She is quick to give credit to her officers for their contributions to the shift. She is always available to assist the officers, but lets them handle incidents and make decisions. She always coaches them in private after an incident that could have been handled better. Most of her officers are good performers, and she will go out of her way to take care of them.

As a matter of fact, that is how you ended up with your split shift. She knew you were a good performer and that you took morning classes at the university, and she is the one who arranged your schedule to accommodate your school activities.

Conclusion Questions:
1. What can be specifically learned from the examples of Brad and Sharon?
2. How do you think Sharon learned to adopt this management style? Is the same true for Brad? If not, how is Brad's training different?
3. What can you take away from this story for current or future use?

CASE 12
Management and Employee Motivation

You are a supervisor for the kitchen stewarding department at a large hotel. You run the early evening shift. You took the shift over about a year ago. Ever since you started, the performance levels have kept getting better. Employee turnover is down, and people from other departments want to work on your shift. Your staff is very culturally diverse, and everyone respects each other. The chief steward, John, is your direct supervisor and is very impressed with the way you run your shift.

During a performance appraisal interview, John comments on how much your staff respects your leadership ability. He says offhandedly, "How do you do it? You have so many individuals from various backgrounds, the work is terribly difficult, and yet they all seem to get along and will set the world on fire for you." You say to him, "It is really just a matter of understanding what motivates people to do good work."

Preliminary Questions:
1. Specifically explain how to understand the motivational factors for people who do this type of work.
2. Are there ways to trigger motivation in people who do this type of work without giving them more money? What might you specifically do in such a situation?

Conclusion: As the conversation moves on, you are ready to provide John with a few examples of how you motivate your workers. "For example," you say, "take this guy—he works two jobs and is going to vocational school. The most important thing for him is to have time to juggle these activities. So, I work with him when it comes to the schedule.

And Sheila over there, she has been dumped on her whole life. All she wants is a little respect, so we all refer to her as "Ms. Sheila," and she loves it. This is in stark contrast to that guy over there. He is basically shy, and when he isn't working he produces great paintings. I don't make a fuss over him; instead I look at his latest paintings and comment on them. Heck, I even bought one of them."

The chief is impressed with your understanding of human motivation. He says, "You know, I hate to tell you this because I wouldn't want to lose you. But the housekeeping director approached me to see if it is okay if she recruits you as an area manager. This would be a promotion for you, and I can't blame you if you decide to talk with her about the opportunity." You say, "Thanks, John. Some bosses would have tried to keep a guy like me from getting promoted just to make their lives easier. I respect you for that."

Conclusion Questions:

1. Is John a good manager, in your opinion? Specifically, why or why not?
2. Would you have done what he did? Are you sure?
3. Do you think most managers would help a good supervisor to get a transfer? Why or why not, specifically?

CASE 13
The Department Transfer

You are an audio/visual (A/V) technician for a convention center. You have been working in the department for about one year. In the past the A/V manager, Matt, has worked around your school schedule. However, two weeks ago your schedule changed, creating conflicts with your classes. You stopped by Matt's office to discuss this, and he kind of blew you off by saying, "Oh yeah, it was just a mistake on the part of the assistant. Work with me and I'll fix it next week." So you worked with him. The next week, the schedule had the same conflicts. You entered Matt's office and he was apparently very stressed. He barked, "I can't do everything for everyone around here! You have to work with me on this." You felt a little disgruntled at this treatment, but you complied with the schedule. Upon arriving at work yesterday, you noticed that your scheduled hours had not changed from last week. Feeling a little uncertain about approaching Matt for a third time, you decide to visit the employee relations manager in the human resources office.

Nadia has just been promoted to employee relations manager from an operations management position. You worked with her when she was a convention services manager and feel comfortable talking with her about your scheduling situation. She listens closely to what you have to say about the past couple of weeks. She leans toward you as you speak, and takes notes. She acknowledges your sentences and paraphrases your descriptions to ensure her understanding of the issues. Her facial expressions demonstrate genuine concern for your situation. She behaves in an objective yet caring manner, and at the end of your explanation paraphrases everything that has happened with the schedule and your meetings with Matt over the past two weeks. She ends the meeting by saying, "Give me some time to discuss this with Matt, and I will let you know what to expect. I will have an answer for you by the time you start work tomorrow, so be sure to visit with me just before starting your shift. Or, if you like, I can call you at home." You agree to stop by tomorrow, and thank her for her time.

After your departure from Nadia's office at about 6:00 P.M., she is ready to leave for the day. On her way out, she stops by the human resources director's office to chat. She says, "You know, I just don't understand it; when I worked in operations I ran around all day long to keep up with everything. Now that I have this job, it seems so much easier since I just sit there and handle people's problems. But when I go home at the end of the day I am totally wiped out—much more so than when I used to run around putting out fires all day long." The HR director gives Nadia a knowing smile and a nod of the head, and says, "You are experiencing emotional energy drain." "What's that all about?" asks Nadia. "Look," the HR director answers, "you sit there all day long actively listening to negative situations. While you think you are doing nothing, by the end of the day you are emotionally and mentally drained from this activity. It's hard work to listen to people's problems." "Oh, I get it," says Nadia. "Brain drain!"

Questions: What factors might have caused Matt to act like a stressed-out manager? Is there anything we can learn from Nadia's new job experience that will help us in our careers?

CASE 14
The Training Scenario

You have just been hired as a reservations (rez) agent at a central reservations center for a cruise line. On your first day of work, the human resources office processes all of your paperwork and provides you with a two-hour orientation program. The program consists of a few outdated video presentations and some general information about the company's history, policies and procedures, and benefit package options. You are then sent to the reservations center to begin work.

As you walk around the halls, you finally find the reservations center after asking for directions from one of the employees in the hallway. As you enter the center, you notice that the room is buzzing with about twenty-five agents seated at open-space desks, wearing headphones and talking with travel agents and prospective passengers by phone. Standing behind every five or so agents is a headset-adorned supervisor who listens in on random conversations. Everyone is working at a frenetic pace, unaware of your presence as you stand near the doorway for what seems like an eternity. You walk farther into the room to ask the nearest supervisor for the manager. Without interrupting her task or acknowledging you, she points over her shoulder to a glass-enclosed office at the rear of the work area. You enter the office through the open door to find a middle-aged woman talking on the phone. She is obviously engaged in a heated discussion with someone else in the organization. Without breaking stride in her conversation, she points at a chair in front of her desk for you to take a seat. As you wait for her phone argument to come to an end, you take note of the disheveled office space with mounds of computer printouts strewn about.

Finally, the woman ends her phone conversation with a threatening comment before slamming the phone receiver down. She looks at you inquisitively, so you say, "Hi, Fran. Remember me? I interviewed with you a few weeks ago." "Oh yeah," she says. "HR finally got you processed, huh? It's about time. It's a madhouse in here!" She presses the intercom button and says, "Frank, come to the office, please." Frank, one of the supervisors, arrives and is introduced to you. You follow him to the work area. He says, "Sit here and watch Mary. She is one of my best agents." Mary says hello and you pull out a notepad. She says, "What are you doing?" You say, "I thought I would take notes." She replies, "Whatever. I wish I had thought of that when I started."

After a few days of this type of "training," you are placed at your own terminal to begin taking reservations.

Questions: Do hospitality organizations really provide this type of poor training? How should it be done differently?

CASE 15
Managers' Reputations

You work for an events management company. You and a coworker from your department decide to take a break in the office cafeteria. You see a few people you know from other departments, so you and your friend join them. They are in the middle of a typical gripe session, and the conversation sounds something like this:

One person says, "You know, I hear that the firm across town is paying 10 percent more for the same job that I do here." "Yeah," says another, "but I hear they work you to death." "Can't be much worse than here," another pipes in. "I haven't had a day off in two weeks." Someone else says, "Well, if it didn't take forever to get some replacements around here . . . I think HR is permanently on vacation." One person says, "Forget HR; my department is the place that really sucks. No resources, bad supervision, infighting, whatever." Another one says, "Well, in my department, only the manager's 'boys' get the goodies." One says, "My manager tries real hard, but she claims the execs won't pay attention to her." Another says, "That's a bunch of crap. There seems to be plenty to go around when it comes time for your manager's bonus."

Finally, your silence is noticeable to the group. Someone asks, "So how about you guys? I suppose you both work in wonderland." You say, "Oh no, we have our problems. Some things get fixed and others don't. But at least our management team is there to listen." One person in the group says, "Yeah, your managers do have pretty good reps around here. Maybe we should all transfer to your department."

Questions: Why do managers engage in such poor practices? What should be done to train managers to act professionally in their jobs?

CASE 16
Coaching, Counseling, and Discipline

You are an assistant beverage manager on a cruise ship. You are responsible for all of the bartenders, cocktail servers, and barbacks on the ship. Like most cruise lines, your vessel flies a foreign flag and your employees are contracted from countries outside the United States. Aboard most ships, a contracted employee who fails to perform would simply be disembarked at the next port. However, your cruise line has a policy of adhering to human resources policies in accordance with U.S. federal law and common management standards within that country. Therefore, you practice coaching, counseling, and progressive discipline with the members of the staff.

On this trip you have a few new cocktail servers. The rest of the staff has been thoroughly trained. One of the new cocktail servers seems to be having trouble doing her job. Also, you have been watching one of the veteran bartenders for quite a while and you suspect he is stealing liquor. Finally, at the beginning of this ten-day trip, a female passenger lodges a complaint with the purser, alleging that another bartender treated her in a rude manner, but she isn't very specific about exactly what he said or did to her.

You decide that you will resolve each of these matters by the end of this trip.

You decide to start with the new cocktail server. Although she managed to pass her training tests, after some careful observation you notice a few problems with her service. For one thing, she has trouble balancing her trays and sometimes topples items. You spend some time with her in a closed outlet to show her how to place items on the tray, balance the tray during her walk to a table, and remove the items from the tray. To avoid any further breakage, you use plastic containers containing water. After a while she gets the hang of tray-handling skills. The next thing you work on is garnishes. The ship serves a number of tropical cocktails requiring various garnishes. You show the server a couple of easy tricks for remembering each garnish, and she soon gets that down pat. The final thing you notice is that she is mixing up her drink order abbreviations, which is causing her to mis-ring items from her order pad, resulting in waste. You review those with her by turning the abbreviations into little memory games. In a couple of days, the cocktail server is almost as good as her veteran peers. She is thankful for the time you spent coaching her.

At the same time, you review the purser's log of the rudeness incident involving one of your bartenders. You note the name of the complaining passenger and visit her to apologize for the incident and to get some specific information. The passenger tells you, "Oh, I am sure it was a misunderstanding, but I think the bartender could have been nicer to me." You then spend some time with the bartender to listen to his side of the story. The two stories match, and you realize he could have done a better job with the passenger. You counsel him on what to do with similar incidents in the future and document your session with a note to file.

Questions: Are there any other issues for you to address in this story? How would you handle them?

CASE 17
The Special Restaurant

You are an assistant manager for a restaurant that is part of a small chain of ten stores. You are attending the annual awards conference for the chain at a beautiful resort. Once again, your restaurant has won the highest achievement award for total revenues and net profit. Many of the employees from your store are at the conference and are rightfully celebrating the victory in grand style. Tonight is the awards dinner to be held in the grand ballroom at the resort.

You are lounging at the tiki bar at the resort recreation area. A couple of managers from other stores buy you a drink. One of them says, "You guys have been winning most of the awards ever since I joined the company. What's up with that?"

You decide to tell your story. "We are not your typical restaurant," you say. "For instance, we don't have bussers, host staff, or barbacks. Everyone takes care of his or her own stations and areas. The managers work the door and the floor. There is no such saying as 'it's not my job' in our store. Everyone is part of the team. The servers have stations, and every one of them makes a minimum of 25 percent of sales as an average. But their job is to roam the rest of the floor to see how they can assist the other guests. If one of them gets in the 'weeds,' they ask for help and the floater is dispatched to them, and servers in the nearest stations also assist them. We don't take breaks during meal periods. If someone needs a break, there is a floater who covers those periodically. The same is true for the income and activities of bartenders. Every person on the culinary team knows every station in the kitchen, and frequently works each one. The same is true for most of the service staff; most of them have completed culinary training. That way they can fill in for the kitchen staff when they get in the weeds. Every manager knows every job in the house; you can't become a manager until you have this ability. We have twice the number of managers of a normal store. But we make so much money that we can afford the salaries, and nobody sits in an office while we are doing business. Our turnover is practically nothing, but when we do need a team member, she or he doesn't interview, but auditions for the job. During his or her audition time (usually one month), every team member votes on whether the person should join us. It is kind of like a fraternity or sorority; you either get 'blackballed' or get voted in."

The managers look at you with mouths agape. "We never heard of such a thing!" "Well," you reply, "buy me another drink and I'll tell you how things got that way."

Question: How would you develop such a restaurant?

CASE 18
Subjective Management Practices

You work as a banquet captain at a local hotel. You have been there for about two years. A new banquet manager was hired about three months ago. Last month the human resources office generated a formal performance appraisal form for the banquet manager to complete. He leaves a copy of the completed form in your mail slot. You review it and are disappointed in his rating of your performance. It is the lowest rating you have ever received. You really aren't sure how to address this issue, so you decide to think about it for a while.

Before you have had a chance to talk with the banquet manager about your performance appraisal, you receive a call from the catering director (the banquet manager's supervisor) to meet with her and the banquet manager in her office at an appointed time.

You arrive for the meeting and take a seat. Joe, the banquet manager, begins to speak to you as Jane, the catering director, observes. Joe says, "Jane informed me that performance appraisals are more involved here than they were at my last hotel. So I did my homework and revised your appraisal. I would like to share my findings with you."

Joe continues, "First, I looked at your personnel file and found many very complimentary guest comments. The guests really love your service, which is a great contribution to the department. Also, I reviewed your former appraisals and noticed that you have consistently been rated as an excellent employee. I compared my observations of your performance to the standards of service for the banquet department, and must admit, you exceed every one of them. So, I would like you to take some time to review my ratings and comments, and feel free to discuss anything you like about your position here."

As you review the form, you think to yourself, "I thought other hotels were as good as this one. I think I'll stay here for a while."

Questions: What steps helped the banquet manager catch his mistakes? If you were in charge, how would you have handled the performance appraisal in the first place?

CASE 19
Job Opportunities

You are ready to graduate from school at the end of this semester. During your school years you worked in front and back line positions at a country club, freestanding restaurant, hotel, and convention center. You received excellent evaluations in all of your jobs. You have the names and contact information for all of your former bosses. Each of them would love for you to join their company as a full-time supervisor after you graduate.

Unfortunately, this situation isn't true for most of your friends. They are hoping to get management jobs when they graduate, but haven't had much experience and don't really even know where to start.

As it turns out, you have decided not to go to work at any of your former places of employment. During your last semester at school you attended a few job fairs, networked with some industry professionals, and developed some wonderful references.

A recruiter for a cruise line got your name from one of your professors who used to work in that industry, and he is willing to hire you in a shoreside marketing position at the company's central office. The job pays well, with great benefits including free travel. Sometimes the job leads come from the most unexpected places.

Questions: Is networking a powerful way to get the good jobs? Why or why not? Identify some of the networking opportunities you have taken advantage of recently.

PART 3
Case Vignettes in Human Resource Management

CASE 20
Human Resource Management Overview

You have just completed your first day as an intern in the human resources office for a large cruise line. You normally work in the reservations department, but after you expressed an interest in learning human resource management, the director arranged for you to do a one-day internship per week. For you, this day has just flown by. The office is a madhouse, with the phones ringing off the hook all day long. Everyone works at a frenetic pace in an effort to handle employment inquiries, pre-employment screening interviews, employee complaints, and demands by the operations managers to fill vacant positions.

At the end of the day, you kick back with a friend to talk about your experience. You remark, "I had no idea that so many things happen in that office. It's even busier than the rez department. I'm not so sure I want to work in this field, it's so negative." Your friend replies, "Give it a chance, it's just your first day. . . ."

Preliminary Questions:
1. Based on experience (your own or the experience of a friend who works in the industry), why do you think this human resources office has so much activity going on?
2. Can you think of ways to make the human resources office environment less hectic? What might they be?

Conclusion: A couple of months have passed since you started your internship in the HR office. You have worked alongside most of the managers and staff who perform various functions. You have gained a little experience in each area of the office. Now you know a little about recruitment and selection, compensation, training and orientation, employee counseling, performance management systems, and legal compliance.

One night you are sitting with your friend, who says, "Hey, how's that internship going? I haven't heard you complain about it since your first day. What did you do, give it up?" "No," you reply. "I'm still doing it and I really like it. I think I want to learn some more about human resources from a management perspective."

Conclusion Questions:
1. Why do you suppose a person would enjoy working in a human resources office?
2. What aspects of this type of work do you find interesting? Why?
3. Do you think it is important for operations managers to have human resource management knowledge? Why or why not?

CASE 21
Recruitment
and Retention

You are a human resources manager for a small chain of restaurants with three stores and about 150 employees. Most of your time is spent with recruitment and selection activities, as well as training. Because your department is small, you don't have a specialist to handle compensation practices. You did, however, participate in a wage and salary survey with the local hospitality HR chapter and learned that you are paying your culinary and kitchen staff at rates below the rates at other restaurants. This explains why you have high employee turnover and difficulty recruiting people for these positions. You dutifully bring this to the controller's and district manager's attention. You explain to them that you would like to propose an increase in wages for these positions to make you competitive in the labor market. They arrange to meet with you in the DM's office the next day.

You arrive at the meeting with Dick, the controller, and Sarah, the DM, armed with your survey data. You begin the meeting with the following observation: "You know, it has been driving me crazy that our turnover rates and recruitment outcomes for these positions have been terrible. Now I know why. We are paying below the rest of the market in this county for these jobs. We need to increase our hourly wages for these positions." Dick looks up from his spreadsheet toward Sarah and says, "This would take us over budget for labor dollars." Sarah glances at you with concern in her eyes. She takes a moment to collect her thoughts, then looks at you and says, "I understand your dilemma. But we made a promise to the owners with this budget. We can't go back to them and say we projected the wrong figures for these wages. They just wouldn't understand. I'm afraid you will just have to do the best you can with our current pay structure."

Immediately upon hearing Sarah's words, you start to become angry. You reply, "If you are so concerned about the owners, what will they say when our turnover costs force our recruitment and training expenses through the roof? Do you know that each hourly position that turns over costs about nine months' wages to replace?" Sarah smiles slightly and says, "Well, those are your budget items, so if that happens, I am afraid you won't meet your budget and that won't look good on your annual performance review." Dick, sensing your vulnerability, chimes in. "That's right, the figures are the figures. You should have asked to change them when we developed the budget." Now you are beginning to seethe at the thought that these two are holding you hostage for trying to do the right thing for the company.

Preliminary Questions:

1. How would you evaluate the attitudes of Sarah and Dick? Do you think they are team players?
2. What would you do about the budget situation if you were the district manager?

Conclusion: Finally, you say, "Well, Dick, looking at these budget figures, it seems to me that you understated the tip credit figures for the servers." Dick stares at you in disbelief. "What are you talking about?" he puffs, as his face turns red. You stare at him with a slight smile. "That's right; the tip credit for servers is off by a quarter per hour per server." You continue, "I wonder what the owners will say when they find that out." Dick says to you, "Why didn't you tell me that before?" You say, "You never asked me, Dick." As they both stare at you, you say, "Seems to me if we correct this little error by the controller's office, we should have more than enough for a wage increase." You stare them both down and casually ask, "Any objections?"

Conclusion Questions:

1. A tip credit permits employers to pay tipped employees less than minimum wage by an amount determined by certain states. By underestimating the allowable tip credit, Dick has budgeted more labor dollars than necessary for tipped employees. What would cause a controller to make such a mistake?
2. Why would you, as a human resources director, be aware of Dick's mistake?
3. Would you have done something differently if you were the human resources director with this company?
4. Do you think this is a good company to work for? Why or why not?

CASE 22
Employee Productivity and Value-Added Management

You are a newly hired assistant manager in the food and beverage department of a large resort. The F&B director holds monthly strategy meetings with all the managers in the department for the purpose of devising new ways of enhancing departmental productivity. At your first meeting, the F&B director has invited the controller and marketing director to participate. You walk in with your manager, grab a cup of coffee, and take a seat. Since you are new to this operation, you observe the dynamics of the following conversations closely.

The F&B director starts things off: "Ladies and gentlemen, I have invited Sheila, the controller, and Mark, the marketing director, to help us with our productivity enhancement initiative. They will provide us with some new ways of looking at our operation." After a preliminary overview of the current status of the initiative, Mark speaks up. "Look," he says, "you've got to spend money to make money. If you want to enhance productivity, you need to drive revenues. The only way to drive revenues is to invest in advertising and promotional activities to increase business." Sheila jumps in. "Hold on there, Mark. The budget is the budget. You don't enhance productivity by overrunning your expense budgets. That's ludicrous," she says. Mark retorts, "Oh, Sheila, not this again. Quite frankly, if you had your way, you would be on the floor with a stopwatch conducting time and motion studies to reduce labor." She defensively replies, "You bet I would! Efficiency is the key to every operation. Our biggest single expense is labor dollars. So, it makes sense to reduce those expenditures as much as possible." Mark says, "Increasing revenues is dollar-wise, and cutting costs is penny-foolish. Put more bucks on the top line and that will take care of the bottom line." Sheila replies, "Mark, apparently you were asleep when they talked about scientific management in your school. If you had your way, we would be out of business."

This discussion continues to go back and forth for quite some time. After a while, you decide to go get another cup of coffee. . . .

Preliminary Questions:
1. How would you describe Sheila's approach to managing resources?
2. How would you describe Mark's approach to managing resources?
3. What thoughts are going on in the minds of the F&B managers as they listen to this argument?
4. Do you tend to agree more with Mark or Sheila? Why?

Conclusion: As you sit down with your second cup of coffee, you begin to realize that this meeting is getting out of control and that this is not the first time that Sheila and Mark have had this argument. The F&B director just rolls his eyes as the two continue to go back and forth with their managerial philosophies. You realize from your training that both Mark and Sheila are correct in their philosophies and that they simply need to put the two concepts together.

Since this is your first meeting, you are a little shy. But after this elongated debate you finally say, "Couldn't we reduce labor costs and increase revenues by developing the talents of our people?" A hush fills the room as everyone turns to stare at you. "Well," you continue, "that would be the human resource approach to enhancing productivity." The F&B director smiles at you with approval. "Next week," he jokes, "we will invite Sheila, Mark, and the HR director to be their referee."

Conclusion Questions:
1. How would you describe the human resource management approach to productivity?
2. Why would a human resources manager tend to be more balanced than the average marketing or accounting manager?
3. What are the pros and cons of Sheila's and Mark's philosophies on productivity?

CASE 23
Legal Compliance

You work in a human resources office for a large resort as a clerical assistant. You are assigned to work with various managers in the specialist departments. Sometimes you work with the training manager, sometimes with the employment manager or compensation manager. When you arrive at work, the director assigns you to work with her on a big project. It seems that an employee has filed a claim of discrimination against the resort. The Equal Employment Opportunity Commission (EEOC) is investigating the allegations and has sent a Notice of Findings of Fact to the human resources office.

You enter the director's office to find that she has already cleared a work space for you. You ask her, "What's the nature of the complaint?" She replies, "You name it; sex, race, color, national origin, and religion." "What?" you proclaim. "How can it be all those things?" The director smiles at you and says, "This is how it is. Once a person becomes a complainant, the EEOC has them complete a checklist of all the factors of discrimination. By the time a complainant leaves their office, he or she has filed a claim based on every form of coverage that exists." You continue to stare at the legal notice in disbelief. Finally you say to the director, "So what do we have to do?" She replies, "Oh, about 100 hours of fact-finding work. We will give the database a workout to pull all of the statistics and reports we will need to defend the organization. It will take us about two weeks to prepare the response." She continues, "Actually, this will be very good experience for you, since you haven't done this type of work yet." She concludes, "So, if you are ready, let's get down to work."

Preliminary Questions:

1. What are the statutes that provide protection to workers based on sex, race, color, national origin, religion, age, pregnancy, and disabilities?
2. Do you think the resort actually discriminated against the complainant, or are there other motives for filing a claim? What might those motives be?
3. Why is the human resources office in the position of having to do so much work to respond to the claim?

Since you began to assist the director of human resources with the response to the EEOC claim, you have learned quite a bit about an employer's burden of proof. It took about two weeks to prepare the Respondent's Report, which consists of about 100 pages of facts, figures, applicant flow data, statistical representation of protected classes, copies of policies, documentation of training sessions, and confidential records of internal investigations.

Conclusion: You are sitting with the director, reviewing the completed report. You say to her, "Is this the end of the matter?" She replies, "Actually, it is just the beginning." You look surprised as you ask, "Well, what happens next?" She sits back; looks upward, as if recalling the last time this happened, and says, "Well, they will take about one month to review our statement. They will call from time to time with questions, which are really ploys to corroborate what we wrote with how we verbally answer the questions. Then we will receive a notice of on-site investigation. An EEOC investigator will arrive about one hour before the agreed-upon time and wander the halls, reading our bulletin boards and talking randomly with the staff members. The person will finally enter my office and request information to, again, corroborate the information in our report. If that goes well, we will be requested to appear at an informal "finding of fact" hearing at the EEOC office. The complainant will be there and will contest our facts. At the conclusion of that hearing, there will be about another month of review, and we will eventually be notified about the status of the claim. The complainant will be issued a Notice of Right to Sue—" "What?" you incredulously interrupt her. "After all that, the complainant receives a right-to-sue notice?" The director smiles at you. "Yup," she says. "It's really no big deal, it is just a notification that the EEOC won't pursue a court trial on the complainant's behalf, but if the complainant wants to proceed to court, that is her legal right."

You sit there, just shaking your head as you listen to the director. Finally you say to her, "I guess that is why we are so careful around here." She smiles and says, "I think you get it. This was a great experience for you, huh?"

Conclusion Questions:

1. Do you think the process outlined above is fair for all parties? Why or why not? Be explicit in your reply.
2. What proactive steps did the resort take before the claim was ever filed? Would the resort be in a position to protect its assets if these steps were not taken? Why or why not?

CASE 24
Employee Relations and Retention

You work in a human resources office for a large resort as a management trainee. Lately you have been assisting the employee relations manager by working as an employee relations representative. In this capacity, you spend most of your day listening to employee complaints about the way their supervisors treat them or interpreting policy issues that they didn't bother to look up in their employee handbooks. You find the work to be emotionally draining, since most of the time you are dealing with negative scenarios. However, it is also rewarding from the aspect of being in a position to help solve disputes and answer employee questions.

At about 3:15, a woman, Bonnie, storms into your office in a fit of rage. Bonnie works as a dispatcher in the room service department on the second shift that begins at 3:00 P.M. She takes over for the morning shift dispatcher, a guy named Bif.

Bonnie slams her hand on your desk and screams, "I've had it with this job! I'm walking out right now. This Bif is a total idiot, and if you don't fire him, I quit! It's him or me, you decide!" she shouts. You look at her calmly and say, "What seems to be the problem?" "What's the problem, what's the problem? I'll tell you the problem. Bif is a creep, a nerd, an SOB, a slob, a derelict, a lazy bum, a stupid idiot, and an ugly, egotistical jerk, that's the problem!" she yells at you. Sensing a potential employee personality conflict, you ask Bonnie, "Have you discussed this with your manager?" She laughs. "My manager? I haven't even seen my manager in three days. My manager, what a joke!"

"I see," you say empathetically. "I'll tell you what. Bif is gone for the day by now. Would you be willing to go back to the room service department and start work to give me an opportunity to look into this for you?" Bonnie replies, "I'll go back there now, but after tonight I'm outta here if you don't get rid of that bum." She leaves your office in a huff.

Preliminary Questions:
1. Identify at least three of the most important observations in this scenario.
2. At this point, what do you think is the cause of Bonnie's behavior?

Conclusion: As soon as Bonnie leaves, you walk into the employee relations manager's office to describe the interaction you just encountered. The wise ER manager says to you, "So what do you think we are dealing with here?" You say, "Sounds like a personality conflict to me." "Maybe," replies the manager. "How about the absence of the room service manager during a shift change, what do you think about that?" You reply, "It seems to me like an important time for the manager to be around, since one shift is closing and another is starting, while the phone keeps ringing. Maybe the manager was called into a meeting or something." "Maybe," says the ER manager, "but your report says that Bonnie hasn't seen the manager in three days, which tells me he hasn't been available for three consecutive shift changes. What do you think about that?" You jokingly reply, "I hate it when you make me think." He chuckles. "I know, but that's my job in training you." You say, "Well, I guess we need to find out why the room service manager hasn't been around for these shift changes." The ER manager replies, "Sounds like a good start."

The ER manager picks up the phone and dials the room service manager. "Hi, Bob. Could you stop by here right away? I think there is a situation you should know about." The room service manager arrives about five minutes later. "What's up?" he asks. The ER manager explains the situation. After citing all the facts, he says, "What disturbs me, Bob, is that when we asked if this complaint went to you, we were told you haven't been around during the shift changes, which is contrary to the policy in our managers' manual." Bob replies, "Yeah, the F&B director has had me putting together a project for the past couple of weeks, and I have gotten so caught up in it that I forget to check with the dispatchers during the shift change. I know exactly what the problem is, and the cause is really not a personality conflict between Bif and Bonnie, it's the overlap situation. Normally I make sure Bif keeps the area neat for Bonnie's arrival. Then I usually have him close out in the service area so he isn't in the booth while she sets up.

To give her a hand, I usually handle the phones for her for about fifteen minutes. Whenever Bif thinks I'm not watching, he leaves Bonnie a sloppy area and makes snide comments to her during the overlap because he knows she has a short fuse." Bob finishes by saying to both of you, "I'll take care of this and let you know when it's fixed so you can check back with Bonnie to make sure everything is all right with her."

"Thanks, Bob," the ER manager says. After Bob departs the office, the ER manager smiles at you and says, "Another day; another experience. Let me know when you get a tough one," he jokes.

Conclusion Questions:
1. Now that you have more information, what would you say if you had to critique the way this situation was handled? Be specific with your comments.
2. If you had to differentiate between symptoms of a problem and an actual problem, how would you analyze this case by listing symptoms and real problems?
3. If you had to place your "core problem" into categories such as human resources, systems, and material resource problems, which categories would apply to the core problem(s) you have already identified?

CASE 25
Employee Retention

You are working as a clerical assistant in the human resources office for a large, internationally recognized theme park complex. One month ago there was a terrorist attack in New York City. Since that time, the theme park has been under high alert as a potential terrorist target. The tourism industry in your town relies heavily on visitors who arrive by air travel. Since the attack, the numbers of arriving air passengers have declined significantly in your city. As a result, visitor volume at the theme parks has dropped by at least 50 percent. Immediately following the attack, the corporate office issued a freeze on all position requisitions. Since that time, all part-time workers have been laid off and full-time workers have had their hours reduced. The big fear among the workers is that a massive layoff of full-time workers might occur.

Preliminary Questions:
1. There are two types of approaches to addressing this problem. A reactive approach would focus on short-term responsive action without concern for long-range complications. Another approach would be to take a proactive stance that balances the immediate responses with long-term concerns. Which approach would you take? Why?
2. The most vulnerable people in this situation are the hourly employees. The salaried managers and professional employees are the most costly, however. Would you consider ways to reduce expenses in the hourly and salary categories? What ideas come to mind to make this happen?

Conclusion: The human resources director has called a department meeting for first thing this morning. All of the human resources managers and workers are present at the meeting. There is a somber mood, as everyone has an idea of what this meeting will be about. The director starts to address the group. "Well, guys, as you know, business isn't getting any better. We have tried every trick in the book to retain our full-timers, but we are getting heat from corporate to start downsizing. I was in the president's office all day yesterday, and the bottom line is that we are being told to reduce the full-time hourly and supervisory staff payroll by 5 percent. I hate the idea of putting our people out on the street, especially now when jobs are so scarce in this town. I called you all together to see if there is some sort of creative solution we can come up with to avoid a massive layoff."

Everyone in the room is silently thinking about the ramifications of a layoff, including concerns about their own jobs. After a long silence, the director chimes in. "C'mon, guys. I know this is not the best of times, but we have a chance to use our talents to do as little harm as possible to our cast members."

You figure there is nothing to lose, so you speak up. "I have a friend who works in general services in the cruise division, and he tells me that they are recovering quickly from the tragedy and that bookings are going through the roof. I guess the guests who would normally visit our parks are opting for cruises, since they seem to be safe vacation getaway options. The hiring freeze has been lifted over there, so maybe we could shift some park personnel to shoreside and onboard cruise positions."

"Hmmm," the director murmurs, "I didn't even think of the cruise division. I'll bet they are doing more business than before the tragedy." The employment manager jumps in by saying, "We can notify everyone of the problem we are facing here in the parks and announce opportunities for temporary placement with cruise operations. I know that they schedule their onboard staff using three-month employment contracts. Usually, they fill the contracts from outside sources. We could offer these contracts to cast members who are flexible enough to work in onboard positions. As far as shoreside jobs, they will just have to work in a different location on a temporary basis."

The compensation manager adds, "Since the cruise division revenues will be higher than budget, they will be able to afford a few extra benefits. We could outsource some of our janitorial and housekeeping staff to one of our vendors to provide housecleaning and lawn maintenance for those cast members who elect onboard temporary positions, and offer that service as a benefit. We can pay for it from one of the benefit accounts, which will be a small amount of the payroll savings due to the outsourcing of our own staff."

The training manager suggests, "We can shift our training resources to cruise operations and get everyone prepared with the necessary skills through 'crash-course' training programs. Since our cast members already know our service basics, all we have to do is brush up on the technical job aspects. We can have them ready to do new jobs in a flash."

At this point, everyone is enthusiastically buzzing with great ideas. The director is visibly enthused and says, "This is a fabulous alternative to layoffs. I'm going to call the cruise division HR director right now."

Conclusion Questions:

1. Do you think it is a good idea to switch workers from the parks division to the cruise division? What are the advantages and disadvantages of this strategy? Be specific.
2. Identify the HR specialists in this scenario and match their ideas to each specialty. Evaluate their contributions to the overall strategy. Explain the value of specialized contributions to general outcomes.

CASE 26
Legal Compliance

You have been working in the human resources office for a large resort for about six months now, performing clerical support functions. During this time you have witnessed the good, bad, and ugly with regard to the skills of various managers through their interactions with the office workers and, in particular, the human resources director. Since you came from working in operations, you already knew which managers had good and bad reputations with the staff. This has only been reinforced through your observations of personnel replacement requisitions, disciplinary actions, and employee complaints. It seems that the managers you heard were bad do turn out to be really bad at managing their staff members.

One of the newly hired department directors is a recent retiree from the Coast Guard. He is in charge of marina operations at the resort. Prior to the retired captain's appointment, an easygoing, nice guy ran the department for twenty years. In the view of the captain, the department was lax and required discipline. His self-appointed mission was to shake up the department by putting pressure on the managers and supervisors. After a few months on the job, the captain drafted a scathing performance review document for his inherited assistant director, a woman who was about thirty-nine years old. In the comments section of the performance review he noted that the assistant's demeanor toward the guests and hourly staff was "brusque and truculent." He went on to write the comment that the only salvation for the retention of this individual would be to send her to "charm school," to alter her behavior to reflect "civilized conduct," as opposed to her demonstrated actions which resembled the activity of an "untethered Sputnik."

Additionally, the captain gave the assistant a "does not meet perform-ance expectations" rating. Up until that time, the assistant had been rated as "excellent" in each of her ten years of employment in the po-sition. The woman, who was somewhat heavyset, became highly agi-tated during the performance appraisal interview with the captain. At one point she jumped up to exit the room and brushed hard against the captain's side, knocking him ajar. She then left the office, jumped into her car, and sped away.

That same day, the captain stopped by the human resources director's office to notify her of the incident. The director advised the captain to contact the assistant by phone at home to inquire whether she planned to return to work on the next scheduled shift.

Preliminary Questions:
1. What are your opinions concerning the actions of the captain? Consider this scenario from both points of view (the assistant direc-tor's and the captain's).
2. Is there a potential for legal action against the resort? Identify the legal foundations of such a potential.

Conclusion: A month has passed since the incident between the captain and his assistant. The captain did call the assistant's house for three days in a row following the incident and left messages asking her if she intended to return to work. She never returned the calls and never returned to her job. After three days, the assistant was considered to have abandoned her job. An employee separation form was completed and a personnel requisition was filed to fill the assistant's position. The captain promoted one of his supervisors to the position, and all was well in the marina operations department—except that the captain received a disciplinary warning for violating company policy by issuing a performance appraisal without the approval of the human resources director.

When you arrive for work this morning the director calls you into the office to work on a project with her. She shows you a letter from an attorney demanding a settlement on behalf of his client, the former assistant to the captain. Attached is a deposition from the assistant not-ing several allegations of improper treatment toward her by the captain.

The claim notes that because of her size and weight, the captain personally disliked her. She goes on to claim that she never intended to leave her job, but the treatment by the captain made life unbearable for her at the resort. In essence, she claims it was a matter of constructive discharge. She goes on to say that she was thoroughly embarrassed by the performance appraisal and was treated outrageously in the appraisal interview process, alleging the captain's intentional infliction of emotional distress on her. As a result, she is unable to gain employment, as she feels faint every time she goes to apply for a new job. She claims she was so traumatized by the captain's treatment that she is under the care of a physician and requires medication to prevent outbreaks of depression and anxiety. Further, she claims that the captain blocked her egress from the office during the interview, substantiating false imprisonment, and that when she tried to leave, he assaulted her. Additionally, she claims that the captain spread false rumors about her among the staff to cast her in a poor light, and that this was a matter of defamation of character by slander. Her knowledge of these remarks further aggravates her medical condition, especially when she reflects on her coworkers sharing information about her poor performance that was found in the captain's office, constituting negligent maintenance and disclosure of records, as well as libel. Finally, her attorney concludes that the actions of the captain traumatized his client to a degree where she is unable to engage in gainful employment, and that he is seeking damages in excess of $500,000 to compensate her for twenty potential years of lost earnings.

After you finish reading the documents, the director gives you one of her knowing smiles and says, "Here we go again. I will need you to put together information to establish evidence that we acted within our policies. This will require document searches and statements from every person in the department. This will take us a couple of weeks." You say to her, "Is this going to be like that EEOC case we worked on?" She replies, "Kind of, but not really. This is a matter of common law." She continues, "In this case, we have to demonstrate that we acted within reason and that she is being unreasonable." Then she glances toward you and says, "You are really getting a lot of experience in a short period of time here, aren't you?"

Conclusion Questions:
1. Based on the facts in this case, match each pertinent allegation with a legal doctrine.
2. How will the investigation associated with this case differ from one concerning an EEOC complaint? Be specific.
3. Is there anything that could have been done before the performance appraisal interview to prevent this lawsuit?

CASE 27
Recruitment
and Selection

You are working as a clerical assistant in the human resources office for a large casino/hotel. You have been assigned to assist the employment manager during the recruiting season that will last for about three months. The employment manager is responsible for all of the planning and implementation of recruiting and selection processes. While you have never worked directly with the employment staff, you have observed that they seem to be always working at a frenetic pace, trying to process large numbers of applicants who appear at the door every day. To you it seems like a very stressful environment, with people scurrying to process all the applicants.

You remember that when you used to work in operations, some of the managers would talk badly about the employment personnel. You recall comments about how they just took their sweet time to replace vacant positions and that they didn't realize how stressful it was to work without those replacements. Back then, you got the impression that the employment people were pretty lazy and didn't really care if a position was placed or not. After all, they always went home at 5:00 P.M., while the operations personnel were still working. But you also remembered your manager as not having any problems finding replacements for positions. In your recollection, your manager would visit the HR office frequently to work on manpower planning revisions, and keep the employment people up to date on any changes in recruitment and selection needs. It seemed that your old department always had a sufficient supply of replacements for vacant positions. So, you wondered, why did these other managers have so many problems?

The employment manager invites you to lunch to familiarize you with his operation. You are sitting together as he presents the stream of activities from recruitment, through selection, to placement of personnel. Afterward, he asks you if you have any questions at this point. You reply, "I am a little confused. When I was in operations there were managers who would complain about how long it took to get a personnel requisition placed. Yet my manager never seemed to have a problem with that. From listening to the other managers, I was under the impression that the employment people sort of dawdled in the process of placing new hires. Now, after watching you guys work, I see you are really stressed out." The employment manager replies, "These are very good observations." He continues, "Employment is one of the most stressful areas of human resource management. That is why the director only keeps a manager in the employment area for one year, and offers us another specialty after that. She knows that after a year, an employment manager is totally fried. As for the opinions of the operating managers," he goes on to say, "those who plan and communicate never have placement problems. This was the case with your former manager. However, most of them just don't get it, so it is easy to complain."

At the conclusion of the lunch, the employment manager says, "So, are you ready for a real HR challenge? If the employment office doesn't challenge you, no HR function will," he jokes as you both head back to the office.

Preliminary Questions:
1. Why do some managers get their replacements immediately, while others don't? Be specific with your answers.
2. Do you think there is a lack of empathy between the operational and human resources departments? What would you do to change that? Be specific with your answers.

Conclusion: The past three months in the employment office have been a real eye-opening experience for you. You have learned that while the activity levels of processing applicants are very hectic, the employment process actually follows a carefully constructed and constantly revised strategic plan. You have learned that professional networking is the most effective recruitment tool for management and service-related jobs. You have also been taught little tricks like watching the walking pace of a housekeeping candidate and leaving a pencil on the floor to see if the applicant will stop to pick it up. You have found out that casino dealers actually audition for their jobs on the casino floor during live table games. You have also learned that all of the background information other than reference checks are handled by areas outside the employment office, so that employment personnel will not have access to that information.

Perhaps the biggest lesson learned is that all that negative talk from the operating managers is the result of their own doing. The smart managers, like your former manager, communicate with the employment manager on a frequent basis. Those who choose to do that have no problems getting their employment needs taken care of. You can't help but wonder why those other operating managers don't take the time to learn some of the tricks you have recently been taught. The other big thing you have learned is the importance of balancing the legal requirements involved with the recruitment and selection process. The employment manager taught you about classified advertisement documentation and applicant flow tracking, as well as techniques for reference checks and chain-of-custody issues. You also notice that the human resources director works closely with the employment manager by meeting every morning and evening to revise strategies.

Finally, you realize that the past three months have just flown by because every day has been filled with activity from the time you arrive at the office until it is time to go home. Now you know why the director gives the employment manager the opportunity to switch to another specialty function each year.

One night you are kicking back with a friend from an operations department. She says to you, "So how's the 'cake job' in recruitment going?" You reply, "You know, I always thought those guys had a cake job, but now I not only know how hard they work, I also know why your manager never seems to have enough staff."

Conclusion Questions:

1. What are your opinions about the employment processes at the resort? What are the implications of these processes in terms of selection, retention, and performance? Be specific with your answers.

2. In your opinion, why do some operations managers fail to plan effectively? What would you do to change this tendency?

CASE 28
Employee Training and Needs Assessment

You are working in the human resources office for a large resort hotel alongside the training manager. The director of human resources enters the office to discuss a situation that recently came up in an executive committee meeting. She tells you and the training manager that the GM is concerned about declining scores in the guest service index (GSI) ratings. She mentions that the GM is adamant that a new guest service training program be implemented immediately for all guest service personnel. The conversation goes on as follows:

Tom, the training manager, says to the director, "You know as well as I do that there may not be a training need as the cause of the low GSI scores. So, we spend a portion of our budget to provide training to all the service personnel and then the scores will remain low, which means the GM will blame us for poor training." "I know," replies the director. "I tried to talk some sense into the GM, but he is in panic mode and won't listen to me." Tom responds, with a little bit of anger, "Well, this puts me in a bad situation, doesn't it?" The director replies, "Look, take advantage of your new assistant here," as she points toward you. "You two can start to put together a training program while conducting a needs analysis at the same time. If you come up with solid proof that this is being caused by some factor other than training, I will go to the mat for you. Will that work?" Tom responds, "Oh, it will work, all right." He then addresses you, smiling. "You are about to learn the first rule about ways to keep your job as a training manager."

Preliminary Questions:
1. Is the training manager in a difficult position here? How so? Be specific.
2. Was Tom wrong to show a little anger at the director's request for a training program? How should he have handled that scenario?
3. Is the GM being unfair? Is the HR director being unfair to Tom? How so? Be specific.

Conclusion: As soon as the HR director leaves the training manager's office, you say to Tom, "Were you really getting angry at her?" Tom replies, "Naw, this is a trick that she taught me, actually. Sometimes you challenge your leader's support to make sure she will back you up. I know if she could have talked sense into the GM, she would have. Sometimes it takes a few days for the GM to come to his senses. This plan just buys us a little time." Tom smirks in a knowing way.

"Let me show you a few tricks," he continues. "First, always have a 'plan in the pocket.'" "What does that mean?" you ask. "Well," he says, "since our most vulnerable measurement in this business is guest service, you always have to have a new way to teach it on the drawing board. I have been developing my next program for a while now. But you don't tell anyone that you have this program in your pocket. That way they will give you a reasonable period of time to come up with one from scratch." He continues, "The second trick for a training manager is to be keenly aware of what is going on in the operating departments. I walk around the property every day and talk with the staff. I know exactly where the cause of this guest service problem lies." You say, "Where is the problem?" He replies, "It's at the front desk during check-in and check-out. The controller ordered a new software package that forces the desk agents to use nine screens for this process, compared with three screens used with the old system. This is causing the guests to wait three times longer for each check-in and check-out process." "Why didn't you just tell the director that?" you ask. "Because," Tom says, "I have to be able to prove it. Otherwise, I am putting our director in an argument with the controller, and she wouldn't win it without proof." You ask the obvious question: "How are we going to prove it?" Tom replies, "I have two words for you: needs analysis. That is always the training manager's proof of problematic causes."

After working through the needs analysis process for a few days, you and Tom complete a report that offers two solutions to the GSI problem. The first proposal identifies Tom's "new" training program and the second proposal suggests taking a "systems approach" to fixing the glitch in the new software. The human resources director presents the proposals at the next executive committee meeting and immediately visits the training office at the conclusion of that meeting.

You and Tom are sitting there as she walks in with a broad smile on her face. "Tom," she says, "you did it again! The AGM confirmed your findings and the focus is totally on the systems problems." She continues, "The GM will stop by to visit you later today to apologize for putting you on this project and to thank you for your analysis." She concludes, with that knowing smile, "Now I am going to lunch with the controller to commiserate with him for being the focus of the GM's wrath this morning."

Conclusion Questions:

1. Are there other causes besides lack of training for performance problems? What might they be, specifically?
2. Would you consider Tom to be good at his job? What specifically has he done to warrant your opinion about this?
3. Are there individuals in executive positions who do not understand the relationship between training and performance? What can be done to change this?

CASE 29
Employee Compensation

You are working as a clerical assistant in the human resources office for a large resort. You have just finished a three-month assignment with the employment manager to assist with their recruiting and selection process. You arrive for work this morning to find the director of human resources in a meeting with the compensation manager and the director of housekeeping. They invite you to join them.

It turns out that they are discussing alternative compensation plans for guest-room attendants. Currently, the attendants are paid an hourly wage. The housekeeping director believes that wages just encourage workers to put in time. She wants to restructure the compensation format to encourage productivity. She starts by saying, "Look, our standard is sixteen good rooms per attendant per day. This is an allocation of thirty minutes per room. I have mostly good people, and I know they can clean a room in less time. But why should they? If they produced clean rooms at a faster rate, their hours would be cut and they would be penalized with less wages." She finishes by saying, "There has to be another way to reward good workers." The HR director has been listening closely, and matter-of-factly says, "This sounds interesting. Give us a few days to come up with something for you."

The housekeeping director leaves and it is just you, the compensation manager, and the HR director in the office. When the housekeeper is out of earshot, the HR director says, "This is exciting! I have been waiting for someone to get creative in one of these departments." She looks at you both. "We have a golden opportunity to do an experiment here." You say, "I guess this will be my new project." The director smiles as she replies to you, "What a wonderful opportunity for you to be creative."

Preliminary Questions:
1. Why are hotel housekeepers and other similar positions paid an hourly wage?
2. Are there alternative forms of compensation? What might they be?
3. Is legal compliance an issue when designing compensation policies? Name the applicable statutes and describe what they cover.

Conclusion: You start working alongside the compensation manager on the new compensation project for the housekeeping department. He lays out the objectives for the project by saying, "Okay, we have to come up with an incentive-based regular pay system that is in compliance with the Fair Labor Standards Act (FLSA) regulations and doesn't increase payroll expenses." You joke, "Sounds easy enough to me." He chuckles, and then says, "Well, it looks like one way to approach this is to structure a piece rate method." "Hmmm," you say. "Instead of paying by the hour, we pay by the cleaned guest room. But, if they clean sixteen rooms in eight hours, wouldn't they be breaking even with the hourly rate, all things being equal?" "That's true," the manager says, "but the housekeeping director is telling us they can clean rooms faster if there is an incentive to do so." You reply, "So we pay them 'X' per room, and if they clean the rooms in less than eight hours, they go home early." You think for a minute and continue, "But if they demonstrate that they can clean sixteen rooms in less than eight hours, why wouldn't we just raise the standard to eighteen rooms in a shift?" "Now you are thinking like a GM," the manager jokes, then continues. "Actually, anyone who has cleaned guest rooms knows that it becomes harder to clean each room as the day goes on. It's kind of like doing bench-press repetitions in the gym; the first few are easy, then as you get tired, it gets harder to push up the bar." "That's true," you say. "The few times I have cleaned guest rooms, my back was aching after just four hours. So we have to build in the assumption that each room gets progressively harder to clean due to fatigue, and if that is true, the seventeenth or eighteenth room is worth more than the first few rooms." The manager quips, "Now you are thinking like Albert Einstein or something." He continues, "You have something here, though. It looks like we should consider a modified piece rate per guest room." You interrupt, "Is that the same as a stratified piece rate?" "Yup," he says. "Stratified, modified, differential . . . they all mean the same thing."

You both stop talking as each of you starts to picture what it is you are trying to create. After a long pause, the manager starts to sketch out the plan on a notepad. You watch as he draws a diagram. "I've got it!" you exclaim. "Let's pay the same piece rate per room, but let the housekeepers bid on how many rooms they want to clean above sixteen rooms. We'll do it like an amateur golf tournament, with A, B, and C flights. C flight will be those who can do sixteen rooms, B flight will be eighteen rooms, and A flight will be twenty rooms. Members of the A flight will earn more than B, who will earn more than C." The compensation manager mulls this idea over, then says, "From a psychological standpoint, the A and B workers would become the elite and the C workers would be viewed by their peers as slackers." He continues, as if in deep thought, "So the C flight workers would strive to be in the B flight and the B flight workers would try to get into the A flight. The C flight workers who can't advance would probably become turnover statistics. But when the word gets out on the street that we pay premiums for people who can clean twenty guest rooms, good housekeepers will leave our competitors and apply for the positions vacated by our slackers."

"I like it," the manager says. "Me too," you reply. He says, "Let's go show this to the director."

Conclusion Questions:

1. If you were to implement this compensation strategy, what would be likely to happen in three months? Six months? One year from the implementation date? Be specific with your answers and consider positive and negative outcomes.
2. What factors would be required for this compensation plan to be FLSA compliant?
3. If you were to propose this plan, what type of reactions might you expect from the controller, GM, AGM, and housekeeping director?

CASE 30
Performance Appraisals and Management Responsibility

You are working in the human resources office for large resort hotel. A worker from the front desk comes into the office complaining that she didn't get her annual wage increase. You ask her if she has talked with the front office manager about it, and she tells you she has mentioned it twice and is tired of asking him for the raise. You ask when her raise was due, and she says it was supposed to start last month. Next you ask her how she rated on her performance appraisal, and she tells you that she doesn't know what her rating was. Surprised, you ask if she had a performance appraisal interview. She tells you that she was called into the office, and was told to sign a form and that she would be getting a raise.

Now you are becoming concerned about this situation. You tell her that you will discuss this matter with the human resources director and get back to her before the end of her shift. She agrees and returns to work at the front desk.

Preliminary Questions:
1. Given the preliminary facts in this case, what do you think happened to cause this situation? Be specific with your answer.
2. Does the scenario in this case present an improper way to handle a performance appraisal? What would be the correct steps for such a process?

Conclusion: After the front desk agent leaves the human resources office, you report your conversation to the director. Upon hearing what you have to say, the director sighs, "I thought this was the case with the front office manager. This will be an opportunity for you to witness the type of conversation you have with a manager who is not living up to his responsibility."

The director immediately calls the front office manager and asks him to meet with her and you. He comes to the office about thirty minutes after the call, and she begins the conversation. "Brad, we have been through this before. You know what our standard is for performance appraisals here. Whether you think it is important or not, you have to follow the process," she says. "I have been more than fair with you on this matter. If you don't want to get with the program, I am going to have to discuss this with your boss." Brad replies, "Look, I know I shouldn't have blown off the last batch of appraisals, but it has been really hectic up there. I just haven't had time . . ." The HR director cuts him off by saying, "Brad, if this was the first time you used this excuse, I would hear you out. But it's not. And you are being irresponsible to your staff, to me, and to this organization. And the worst part is, your employee should have gotten a raise over a month ago, and you never even turned in the form." Frustrated with this conversation, Brad says, "So, what do you want me to do?" The director replies, "I want you to process the payroll change form, go to the accounting office and get a manual check cut for this young lady, sit down with her and tell her what she does well and what she can do better, and apologize for the payroll mistake by the end of her shift." Brad retorts, "I will need the AGM's approval for a manual check! That will make me look bad." The director replies, "You already look bad to your employees, who are more important than your boss. Would you rather have me call the AGM to discuss your mismanagement practices?" she threatens. "No," he replies, "I'll handle it." "Good," the director says. "And when you finish with the employee, send her to see me, so I can check up on the way you handled it. And finally, Brad," she warns, "you either get with the program or I am going to come after you. Do you understand me?" He replies, "I got it," and leaves the office in a huff.

After Brad's departure, the director says to you, "Go on up to the front desk and let the young lady know that things will be taken care of by her manager, and ask her to see me when she is finished meeting with him." You salute and say, "Yes, ma'am!" She laughs. "Well," she says, "sometimes you've gotta get tough with these guys. Now you know how to handle one of these situations."

Conclusion Questions:
1. Was the HR director being too tough with Brad in this case? Why or why not, specifically?
2. Why did the HR director insist that a manual check be cut for the front desk agent before the end of her shift?
3. Do you think Brad's excuse for blowing off the performance appraisal was legitimate? Why or why not, specifically?

CASE 31
Management Communications and Employee Relations

You are working alongside the employee relations manager in the human resources department for the cruise line division of an internationally known theme park and attraction organization. As is the case with most cruise operations, there are individuals from diverse ethnic backgrounds in the shipboard aspect of the operation. Most of the captains and deck and engine crew are European, as are the food and beverage personnel. Onboard hotel managers are mostly from the U.S. and England, and the crew are from Caribbean and Asian nations.

You notice that the employee relations manager works on board for at least four days per month. After watching the employee relations manager handle a number of complaints from shoreside personnel, you notice that most of these boil down to communications breakdowns. One day you ask the employee relations manager how he handles communications with the diverse onboard personnel. He says, "Come on board with me next week and I'll show you."

Preliminary Questions:
1. Why is it that many complaints arise from communications breakdowns?
2. Are there other reasons for employee complaints? What specific categories might include these?
3. Why do you think the employee relations manager goes on board every month?

Conclusion: After boarding the ship, your only task is to follow the employee relations manager as he makes his rounds. You notice a small office with a title on the door that says "Ombudsman." The employee relations manager explains that he places one person on each ship to handle complaints and disputes. This person is called the ombudsman, which is an old term used to describe a neutral party who hears complaints. He goes on to tell you that the ship's captain is the supreme decision maker while the ship is at sea. The ombudsman listens to complaints and grievances of shipboard personnel to assist the captain in handling such matters. Also, the ombudsman relays the information to the employee relations manager so that he may advise the captain in certain important matters.

While looking around inside this tiny office on board the ship, you notice printed materials that replicate all of the items in the shoreside HR office. However, these are printed in multiple languages to accommodate the diverse workers on the ship. After spending four days at sea, you have observed that the only activity performed by the employee relations manager has been to walk the decks and talk with the staff (who all seem to know and like the manager).

At the conclusion of the trip, you ask the employee relations manager, "Why do you go to sea every month? It seems that the ombudsman handles all of the disputes and complaints and all you do is walk around shaking people's hands." The employee relations manager says to you with a smile, "Communication is not always about writing and speaking. The most important form of communication is showing that you care, just like we say we do in the handbooks. When these people see me on board once a month, it reinforces the fact that I care enough to be out there with them, which makes them feel like I am keeping tabs on their fair treatment while they are at sea. Between that and the presence of my onboard ombudsman, the staff feels secure in knowing we are safeguarding their fair treatment, no matter what country they are from. This," the manager concludes, "is called proactive employee relations."

Conclusion Questions:

1. What is the specific difference between proactive and reactive employee relations practices?
2. If you were the employee relations manager, would you go to sea every month? Specifically, why or why not?
3. What traits would comprise the ideal ombudsman on a ship? Be specific.

CASE 32
Leadership Development

You are working in the human resources office for a large branded chain hotel at the property level. The director of human resources invites you to attend the local Hospitality Human Resource Association chapter meeting after work. You realize this is a good opportunity to network with other HR practitioners. You arrive at the meeting and are introduced to the other attendees, who include directors as well as HR specialist (compensation, employee relations, training, labor relations) managers.

The topic of the meeting is leadership strategies. A guest speaker provides a presentation on leadership development programs. After the presentation, there is an open forum discussion session. Since you want to learn as much as you can about HR practices, you pay close attention to the interactions of the discussion session. You start to notice after a while that these HR managers, while somewhat knowledgeable, seem to be lacking some quality that your director has.

Preliminary Questions:
1. Is there a difference between those who possess leadership knowledge and those who actually practice leadership? What specific behaviors would indicate such a difference?
2. Do you think hospitality companies give the title of "lead" or "leader" to individuals with no leadership skills? Provide a specific example of this in practice.

Conclusion: At the office the next morning, you are having coffee with the training manager. You start to tell him about your experience at the association meeting. You then ask, "Is it me? Or is there some quality that our HR director has that the other practitioners don't have?" He just smiles at you.

Finally you say to the training manager, "Are you going to just smile at me? Or are you going to explain why I am sensing a difference between our leader and the other members of the association?" He laughs. "You just answered your own question." "What are you talking about?" you say. He replies, "The difference is leadership. Our director is a leader." He continues, "I have worked with her for some time now. When I started with her, she used to drive me crazy by never giving me direct answers to my questions. She seemed to take almost sadistic pleasure in watching me try things and fail. Some days she would be very nurturing, and on other days she would be a hard-driving task master. I thought she was bipolar in the beginning." The training manager pauses in his own reflection on the past. "Then it dawned on me—she was a leader who was teaching me, in her own twisted way, to become a leader just like her." He smirks a little, and then continues, "As soon as I achieved that awareness, she told me that I was now 'getting it.' It was like she was reading my mind." He concludes, "She and I have been leadership partners ever since."

"Wow," you say to him. "How do you get that way?" He replies, "I don't know, but if she takes you under her wing, you will know you have reached leader status when she no longer appears to you to be the director from hell." He laughs.

Conclusion Questions:

1. Why did the leader act inconsistently when she first started developing the training manager?
2. Was the leader really being sadistic, or was she trying to get the training manager to think for himself? Provide a specific example of how this might work.
3. Was the leader really reading the training manager's mind, or was she just tuned in to leadership thinking? How can this be so?

CASE 33
Employee Motivation and Recognition Programs

You have been working in a human resources office for a large, exclusive resort and vacation ownership organization nestled in a very upscale private living community. A new human resources director has been hired to head the department. You aren't sure why the last director left, but it seemed he just sort of disappeared one day.

The last HR director developed an employee recognition program that calls for guests of the resort to vote for an employee who provides excellent service. The guests are asked to drop a guest service ballot in a large, locked box next to a shiny new two-seater sports car located in the center of the lobby. The estimated value of the car is $35,000, and a large sign is on display that says, "One of our staff associates will win this car based on your ballot demonstrating excellent service." Needless to say, the guests are impressed with this gesture. They think the management team at the resort must be wonderful to award such a prize to an employee.

Preliminary Questions:
1. Do you think this resort is very generous with its incentive program for the associates? Specifically, why or why not?
2. Would you be motivated to provide excellent service based on this recognition program? Why or why not?

Conclusion: After one week of observation and individual meetings with each HR practitioner, the new director calls a meeting with all of the HR staff. After some preliminary items of discussion, the director asks, "Whose idea was it to do this car recognition thing?" One of the staff members says, "I think it was the last director and the executive committee." The director responds, "Bad idea, don't you think?" After a long silence, one of the staff members voices an opinion. "I think we could have come up with something that would give a lot more motivational bang for $35K." Another staff member chimes in: "This program means nothing to the staff. They think it is a joke." She continues, "This is just a PR thing to make the guests think we are generous employers."

After many more opinions along this line, the new director says, "I'm glad to hear you share the honest truth." She continues, "Did you share this information with the past director?" Most of the staff look downward and smirk. Seeing this, the director says, "Let me guess: You were never asked for an opinion." Everyone starts laughing at the obvious truth. "Well," says the director, "there is nothing for us to do now but watch this whole program blow up in the executive committee's faces. It is apparent that whoever designed this scheme knew nothing about the human needs of our staff." Everyone at the table nods in agreement.

The big day finally arrives: It is the end-of-season employee recognition ceremony. With the help of the HR staff, the new director manages to put together some very enjoyable activities including an employee breakfast, barbecue, and dinner. Now it is time to award the sports car. The car is on a huge platform, and a barrel consisting of all the guest ballots for the whole season is prepared for the drawing. The resort president draws a ballot out of the drum and announces the name of a housekeeping attendant.

It turns out that the winning housekeeping attendant is an elderly lady who recently immigrated to the U.S. She is a single head of household with five children. She has no driver's license. When her name is called, she is brought onto the stage to receive the car keys. As the executives look on, they think she is crying tears of joy. In reality, she is scared to death because she doesn't have a clue as to what to do with this two-seater vehicle that she doesn't even know how to drive. You and your colleagues from the HR staff just stand there and shake your heads, thinking about the great program you could have put together with that money.

The story does have a happy ending, however, at least for the housekeeping attendant. The new HR director convinces the executive committee to return the car to the dealer, which yields about one-third of the original value of the car, and that money is eventually awarded to the housekeeping attendant after taxes are taken out. She uses the money for a down payment on a little house in another town, where she takes a job with another resort.

Conclusion Questions:

1. How does this story specifically relate to what you know about worker motivation?
2. Describe how you would use this money to develop a great recognition program for the staff.
3. What do we now know about the mentality of the executive committee at this resort?

CASE 34
Starting and Running an HR Office

You have been working in the human resources office at a large resort for about two years now. During that time you have worked along with managers in each of the specialist functions. You have assisted the employment manager with recruitment and selection activities. The compensation manager has worked with you to devise alternative direct pay processes to standard hourly wages. You have assisted the training manager with employee orientations and have even developed a couple of training programs on your own. The employment relations manager has showed you the ins and outs of handling complaints, as well as employee counseling and discipline. You have even worked alongside the human resources director to handle a few legal compliance issues. So far, it has been a great experience.

The human resources director asks you into her office to discuss an "opportunity," which usually means a new problem. However, this won't be the case today.

She begins, "After working with all of our HR specialists, you now have an inventory of skills to qualify as a human resources generalist. You have done a great job in our department and there is an opportunity that is just right for you." You look attentively at her as she continues, "We have just acquired the small property next door. It is a good strategic move for us, as it gives us additional beach access. The property has about ninety employees. Our executive committee will direct all of the functions at the property, so I will be in charge of the human resources function there." She continues, "I am offering you the position of human resources manager for this property. It will be you and an administrative assistant." She concludes, "Are you interested?"

Preliminary Questions:

1. If you had this experience coupled with the knowledge from your courses, how would you feel about being given such an opportunity? Specifically describe the emotions you would experience in such a meeting, such as joy, apprehension, elation, confidence, etc.
2. What steps would you take during the first 30, 60, 90, and 180 days in this new assignment?

Conclusion: It has been about a year since you took over the human resources function at the little property with ninety employees. Things are running quite well. You have a very good recruitment and selection process in place; you have drafted managers' manuals, policy manuals, and SOPs for all operating areas. Your retention strategies are paying off with low employee turnover and an excellent management team. The property now adheres to a proactive code of ethics, and your legal compliance is impeccable. There are training programs ranging from general orientations through management development programs. You have initiated some very nice performance-based incentive programs, which encourage all members of the staff to be "value-added" workers, with these behaviors also being rewarded through your performance management system.

The human resources director is very pleased with the way you have developed the human resources function at this property. You are proud of the job that you are doing, and you really feel like you are making a difference in the lives of the staff at your property. This alone makes your hard work all worthwhile.

Conclusion Questions:

1. Now that you know what you know, in what specific ways are you a different person than you were at the beginning of this semester?
2. How will this change in your "being" serve you in the future?

PART 4
Hospitality
Operations Cases

CASE 35
The Invisible Car

It is the weekend of New Year's Eve. A young couple from a major metropolitan city decide to have a New Year's Day party instead of a New Year's Eve party. They decide to do this because the wife has to work on New Year's Eve until 2:00 A.M. at a local nightspot. Her best friend from work phones her around 3:30 P.M. on December 30. The caller says, "I'd love to come to your party, but my car is in the shop and it will be there until Tuesday. I have to call in sick tomorrow night as well, and I know our boss is going to be so upset with me." The wife says, "Why don't you rent a car?" The answer: "Well, I don't have a credit card." "No problem," says the wife, "we'll rent one for you so you'll have it all weekend—consider it a little gift."

The couple takes their friend to a major car rental agency in an off-airport location. A compact car is rented at an incredibly low special weekend rate. In this particular state, proper identification of the renter (the husband, in this case) needs to be provided, since he is placing the charge on his credit card and is going to be listed as the primary driver. The wife's friend also shows proper identification and is listed as an additional driver in accordance with the car rental company's policies and procedures. The wife kisses her friend goodbye and says, "I'll see you at work! Then, we'll party the next day!"

New Year's Eve turns out to be a great night for both of the ladies. Working in a popular local nightclub as cocktail servers, they each make over $500 in tips this evening, and both leave to go home and get some sleep for the party on the next day. The rental car, it turns out, is a great gift indeed, since the friend is able to earn over $500 and not have to call in sick for work.

The husband, John, awakens his lovely wife, Linda, with a kiss to celebrate New Year's Day. It is already 12:35 P.M. They need to clean their house thoroughly, confirm the delivery time of the food from the caterer, decorate the front walkway, and make sure the DJ has all the CDs they have requested. Indeed, it is going to be a busy day. The couple leave to complete their long list of errands.

Around 4:14 P.M., Linda's cell phone rings; it is someone crying hysterically, with loud sounds of sirens and traffic in the background. At first Linda has no idea who it is and thinks it is the wrong number. Then, suddenly, she realizes that it is Roberta, her best friend from work. Roberta is crying in such a hysterical manner that Linda cannot understand a word she says. "Calm down!" Linda tells her. "What's wrong?" A man grabs the phone from Roberta and says, "Hello, Linda. Your friend has been in an accident here at Lincoln Drive and Amherst Street. She is uninjured, but visibly shaken. Could you please come to pick her up? Her car has been totaled and she has no means of transportation to return home." With that, the unidentified man hangs up the phone.

What transpires next will affect John and Linda for almost two decades. While their friend Roberta was sleeping late (after working into the wee hours on New Year's Eve), her brother, Frank, took the rental car out for a spin. He did so without permission. Frank was not listed on the rental car agreement. He noticed the car in the driveway and saw the keys on the kitchen counter. Instead of disturbing his sister from her sleep, he decided to just take the car and go for a drive. While he was driving through the intersection of Lincoln and Amherst, an uninsured motorist driving without a driver's license ran a red light and slammed into Frank. The impact was so severe that the rental car was completely totaled. Miraculously, Frank was uninjured. The police went to his house and retrieved Roberta to bring her to the accident scene.

At first, Linda and John feel that it will all be resolved quite easily. After all, they have paid extra to insure Roberta as an additional driver, and have even paid the high fee of $8.95 per day plus tax to purchase the additional insurance so that no deductible will be required in the event of an accident. They calm down both Frank and Roberta and agree to get the party started and not worry about a visit to the car rental agency until the next day. The car is towed away. The police give them the report. The agency is closed, as it is past their 6:00 P.M. closing hour. John leaves a message for the agency manager, stating that he will be there tomorrow. The four of them leave for the party feeling relieved that all will be handled with ease.

As the story unfolds, the facts become quite clear—and they are different from what anyone had originally perceived. First, the uninsured, unlicensed driver was at fault, as he ran the red light.

However, there is no insurance plan from which to recover damages, as he does not have car insurance, nor is his car registered in the state. With further investigation, it is determined that this individual is in the United States illegally and has already received deportation papers. He has no job, has no bank account, and is living on money borrowed from family members to live day to day.

The car rental agency states that the value of the car (which, by the way, was brand new and had only five miles on it when rented) is $14,975. They state that the insurance John and Roberta purchased will *not* cover damages as she was not driving the vehicle at the time, nor was John. Rather, her brother Frank was the driver, and he was not included on the rental agreement or the insurance.

The primary renter, John, calls his insurance agent at a major U.S. insurance company. The agent says that although John has never had a claim and has been an outstanding client, they will not cover the claim as he was not in the vehicle at the time of the accident.

John is being forced to pay the total value of the car plus towing fees by the car rental agency, and they want to collect immediately. As a matter of fact, the car rental company places the entire charge on his VISA account on January 3. John is furious, as this uses all of his $15,000 credit limit on his credit card. He calls VISA to decline the charges, and they refuse.

Tensions start to mount, and Frank and Roberta soon stop returning calls to their "friends," John and Linda. Roberta asks her restaurant manager to change to the day shift so she will not have to see Linda at work any longer.

John seeks legal counsel from one of the top law firms in the city. The attorneys discuss a possible solution with the car rental agency's manager, attempting to persuade him invoke use of the agency's own "fleet insurance" (which covers all cars they own) to recoup their loss and not to seek damages from their client, John. Instead, John will offer to pay them $1,000 in good faith for lost rental revenues and towing costs. All seems in order to save John; however, at the last minute the legal department of the car rental agency's home office responds with an adamant "no," stating that all charges are due as indicated. They will make no concessions and make no bargains whatsoever.

In the end, the uninsured illegal alien motorist who caused the accident flees the country. After having their assets and income analyzed by the law firm, Frank and Roberta are deemed "impoverished" and unable to pay anything near the full amount. They settle for a total of $650. Legal fees come to just under $5,000.

In the end, John pays a total of $20,220 for a car that he never rode in, never drove, and never held in his possession. He secures a ten-year loan to get an interest rate of 9 percent, which is lower than his credit card rate of 18 percent. With interest, he pays a total of almost $30,000 for this horrible experience. Linda's "friend," Roberta, disappears completely from the picture, as does her brother. She quits her job, moves out of state, and only pays the $650 for which she and her brother were found liable—never speaking to John or Linda again.

Faced with this incredible hardship, John does everything in his power to spread bad publicity about the car rental agency which still, to this day, advertises that its customers are "number one" and that it "strives for excellent guest satisfaction." As a business executive, John travels considerably and continues to let people know how this particular hospitality company was far less than "hospitable" with his personal situation.

To this day, over two decades later, everyone in John and Linda's circle of friends refers to this story as *The Invisible Car.*

Questions:

1. Should people not do favors for friends?
2. Should the car rental company have followed a "good faith" procedure and paid for the complete loss? If not, for a portion thereof? How much? Why do you feel that way?
3. Do you feel the car rental company acted properly by protecting its asset? What if John did not have available credit on his credit card at the time of the incident?
4. What would you do as a car rental agency manager to prevent this type of scenario from happening in the future to other clients?
5. What is/are the main issue(s) in this case?

CASE 36
Taking Care of the Elderly

Many university towns face supply-and-demand issues during special events affiliated with the local educational institutions. In this instance, a large land-grant institution is having its annual spring graduation weekend in early May. The university graduates approximately 5,000 students each spring. All hotels in town, as well as in surrounding areas, are completely sold out for this busy weekend. Hotels appreciate the year-after-year influx of family and friends for this special occasion and almost always make considerable revenues, not only from guest rooms but also from restaurant, bar, and gift shop sales.

On this particular weekend, the general manager of the full-service hotel in question is on duty himself. Most guests have arrived on Friday evening; hence, both Saturday morning and Saturday afternoon are quite slow, as the visitors are on campus attending the graduation ceremonies. The manager is having a rather uneventful day when he is called to the front desk by a clerk at around 12:20 P.M. for a problem with a guest regarding check-in.

Upon his arrival at the front desk, the general manager encounters Mr. Sheldon Firestone, an elderly gentleman. Sheldon yells at the GM before he can even extend his hand to introduce himself, snapping, "Why is your staff so ignorant at this hotel? I just want to check in!" After discussing the situation with the front desk clerk, the manager finds out that Mr. Firestone and his wife are the grandparents of a Julia Firestone, who is graduating. Mr. Firestone was suffering from chest pains the prior evening; thus, he was unable to check in Friday night as originally planned, and postponed his drive to the hotel until Saturday. The rest of the Firestone family checked into their entire block of rooms—six rooms in all—Friday at 4:15 P.M. One of these rooms is supposed to be occupied by the elderly couple now attempting to check in. However, there are no names listed with each individual room. All rooms were held under the name Samuel Firestone. Samuel Firestone, the older gentleman proclaims, is his son.

The desk clerk did the right thing by not allowing the elder Firestone to check in, as there is no reservation pending for a Saturday arrival, nor was there any notification that Samuel's father would be arriving a day late. There was no key left for him, there were no messages left in the property management system, and there was no indication of a Saturday arrival in the original reservation. According to hotel policy, the front desk clerk did the right thing by not checking this person in and, instead, conferring with the manager on duty.

The elder Firestone asks if the manager will call his son's cell phone, and provides the phone number to the GM. The GM phones the number provided, but there is no answer and no voice mail. He tries several times over a period of one hour while the gentleman and his wife become quite irritated. Later on, Mrs. Sheldon Firestone finds the phone number for the younger Firestone's wife, their daughter-in-law, Carrie. When they phone Carrie on her cell phone, there also is no answer, but this time there is indeed a voice mail. The recording says: "Hi, you've reached Carrie and Samuel. Please leave a message at the beep." The GM leaves a message. Thirty minutes later he phones again; once again, he leaves a message.

As time passes, the gentleman and his wife become belligerent and combative. They demand to be let into *any* of the six rooms, assuring the manager that they can even identify personal articles once they see them. Sheldon Firestone begins to complain of chest pains and says that if he has a heart attack of any kind, he will sue the manager, the front desk clerk, the hotel, and its owners for not allowing him to enter a guest room which was indeed paid for and already checked into by his own "flesh and blood."

At 5:00 P.M., the Firestones are still in the lobby and begin to yell at anyone walking by—using profanity. By this time the desk clerks have changed, with one shift ending at 3:00 P.M. and another beginning at 3:01 P.M. Theo, the relief desk clerk, asks the couple to please calm down and to please stop cursing. Sheldon responds by spitting on him. As Theo threatens to quit, the general manager calms down the group and states that he will call both cell phones one additional time. Again, the son's phone has no voice mail. This time, however, he leaves a message on the daughter-in-law's phone stating that he can no longer wait for them to return and that the senior Mr. Firestone is so irritated and acting so out of control that he (the manager) is going to permit him to enter one of the rooms.

Upon inspection of all six rooms, the general manager does indeed find one room with personal belongings. There is even a card left on the stand, and on the outside of the envelope is written a statement: "Welcome Grandma & Grandpa." "This *must* be your room," the GM states confidently. He again apologizes for simply following procedures and leaves the elderly couple to rest and wait for their family's return.

After a long, tiring day, the manager leaves for home at 7:30 P.M. Around 8:15, Theo from the front desk phones the GM at home. When the GM answers, Theo sounds shaken. There is a man yelling in the background and threatening to have the GM fired and to sue him for violation of state law. When handed the phone, the upset individual identifies himself as Samuel Firestone, the son of Sheldon Firestone. He proceeds to scream obscenities at the GM and states that the GM has violated laws of the state by admitting someone into their rooms without permission. The general manager attempts to calm him down by saying that he has done the right thing by not having his elderly father suffer any longer in the lobby. The irate younger Firestone will hear nothing of the sort, and says that he is calling the police and filing charges. The GM quickly returns to the hotel. He has never experienced such a situation. How could a guest be so upset with him for doing the right thing and assisting his own elderly father into a room? Could he have violated a law?

By the time the GM returns, the police are there and they are completing a report. The man continues to yell and threaten, although with the police officers present, he does not use obscenities. The GM once again apologizes and says that it is indeed policy not to permit entry into rooms without picture identification matching the name on record of a reservation, but that the elderly couple had waited over four hours and were in need of a rest. Furthermore, there was even a card left for them indicating that they were the Firestone party meant for that vacant room. The son will hear nothing of the sort. He refers to a state law that says innkeepers cannot ever allow anyone entry into a room without exact identification matching the name on record. The son starts to dial his personal attorney on his cell phone while the police officers are finishing up their report. When the GM tells the police officers that the elder Firestone spat on his employee working the front desk, the police officers seem to side with the Firestones, and only document the statement after considerable persuasion from the GM.

After departure of the law enforcement individuals, the GM is asked to speak to a Mr. Patrick Rexler, attorney for the Firestone family.

He informs the GM that he has indeed broken the law and that if he doesn't want the Firestones to press charges, he must refund all room and tax charges for all six rooms for both nights. Additionally, he suggests reimbursing the family for their "pain and suffering" by including at least one full dinner for the entire family (a party of eighteen), and quite possibly even a complimentary future two-night stay. The GM says that the demands seem excessive since he was attempting to accommodate the guests and did the right thing. Mr. Rexler says, "Have it your way. I'll start the paperwork on Monday." The GM responds, "No, sir, I understand you're speaking of the law and you sound quite serious." The attorney responds, "The right thing doesn't always mean it's the legally right thing."

The refunds are given. In total, the hotel loses revenue on six rooms for two nights each. The rooms rented for $159 per night per room during graduation weekend plus taxes, for a total loss of $2,098.80 (6 rooms × 2 nights × $159/night per room + 10% tax). Additionally, the family is provided with a full four-course dinner, including beverages. The dinner would have cost $785 if it were paid for by the family. Using a food cost of 34 percent and a labor cost of 20 percent, the real cost of the dinner to the hotel is $423.90. Furthermore, the family occupies the tables during a sold-out graduation dinner period for the hotel, which causes additional lost revenues by the restaurant not being able to turn the tables two times. The younger Firestone tells the restaurant servers that he and his family are relaxing, taking their time, and making up for the hotel's lack of respect for his family. Lastly, the family does not provide any gratuity to the servers, and that adds an additional $150 in cost as the GM feels obligated to compensate his employees who have been "stiffed" by the Firestone party. A total hotel loss of $2,672.70 has been incurred.

Questions:
1. What is the major issue in this case?
2. Would you have acted in a similar manner as the general manager? Why or why not? Is it okay to "do the right thing"?
3. What are the laws and statutes in your particular state about such scenarios? Do you agree with these laws as written? Why or why not?
4. What if a lower-level manager had been involved in this instance? Do you think the attitude of the family involved would have been different? Why or why not?
5. What internal policies or procedures should be changed so that this type of scenario does not reoccur?

CASE 37
There's a Mouse in the House

The lobby is full, with over 100 people milling about. It is a Sunday in April, the height of the season for this destination. With a major attraction just one mile away, the lobby is packed with guests desiring to check out at 9:00 A.M. All three clerks have lines with at least ten guests waiting to check out. There are kids sitting on suitcases, the concierge is explaining directions, the manager on duty is boarding people on the courtesy shuttle, and even the chief engineer is there, chatting with a family about typical weather for this time of year.

Suddenly, a screaming woman appears on the scene. Yelling so loudly as to stop all other conversations, she runs toward the front desk, swinging a plastic bag above her head. "Look at this! Look at this, you people!" Everyone turns to look in disgust as the ranting and raging woman hurtles toward the front desk with a dead mouse in a plastic ziplock bag.

"We refuse to pay! This mouse was in my bed! This hotel is a disgrace to everyone and anyone in this community. Someone please call the police!" The front desk clerk she approaches, Rafael, is completely caught off guard. Mrs. Johnson, the guest he was originally checking out, moves away from the desk to allow for the ensuing performance. "I'm Rebecca Peterson in room 320!" screams the lady with the mouse in the bag. "This dead mouse was in our bed this morning when we woke up, and we refuse to pay!" With that, she throws the bag at Rafael and storms out of the lobby. One guy in line says, "Yeah, we need a discount too. We had a dead cow in our room." "I don't like the food here. Give me $50 off my bill," another belts out.

Several guests begin to laugh. Several mention that maybe the mouse is a mascot from the nearby petting zoo. Some say that it probably died after it ate the free continental breakfast. By this time, the manager on duty, Ginny, is by the side of Rafael with the lifeless mouse in its plastic home. Order slowly returns around the lobby, and within thirty minutes the crowd is gone—on their way to the attractions, to the beaches, to the shopping malls, or returning to their homes.

Ginny feels horrible about the situation, although she has to laugh. The entire staff has already heard the rumors, and various accounts of the incident have spread like wildfire through the corridors, from the housekeepers to the pool attendants. The mouse now even has a name: It is Pepper, because, it is assumed, he or she likes pepper jack cheese. Instead of bothering the GM at home, Ginny agrees that it is useless to do anything more about it. She adjusts off the entire charge for room 320. The Peterson party has been at the hotel for four days and three nights and has several restaurant, gift shop, pool bar, and movie charges. Ginny unhappily adjusts off over $2,000 from the hotel's revenues.

On Monday, Jeremy, the general manager, arrives to find an in-box full of papers and forms, which is quite normal after a busy weekend. However, he also sees a plastic bag stuffed into his box. To his dismay, he pulls out the bag and finds "Pepper." Hysterical laughter fills the executive office when everyone realizes that Jeremy has found a new friend.

Jeremy reads the attached incident report and can't help laughing hysterically. After all, it is funny in a way. He immediately phones the chief engineer, the pest control company, and the manager on duty who had worked that morning (Ginny). While waiting for people to arrive in his office, he notices something strange about Pepper. There appears to be a weird look to his skin. Jeremy becomes irate when he opens the bag and realizes that Pepper is nothing more than a plastic toy mouse from a pet store. Underneath his belly is a sticker that reads, "A Cat's Best Friend—Made in China." The office goes silent.

Jeremy quickly places the full charges back on room 320's guest folio and calls the credit card company to make sure there is a notation that the guests cannot dispute the charges at a later time. About one month later, Jeremy receives an irate call from a Mr. Peterson who says, "How dare you charge my credit card! My wife and I stayed there a month ago and we found a mouse in our bed! Take those charges off immediately!" Jeremy replies, "The mouse was a fake—you know it and I know it! You might want to check with your credit card company; they know the truth. Would you like to see the photographs? I have already reported you to guest relations of our worldwide hotel chain so it will be duly noted in the event you again try such a scam at another property." With that, Mr. Peterson hangs up and is never heard from again.

Questions:
1. Is there anything that the front desk could have done differently during this scene?
2. Is it possible for guests to try such outlandish things? Why or why not?
3. Was Ginny at fault for not doing a proper investigation? Should it have been handled differently?
4. What can you do as a manager to protect against such scenes in your lobby?
5. Do you think the other 100 people in the lobby who were checking out at the same time will have their perceptions of this hotel permanently changed? Should other discounts have been provided to these guests to promote "goodwill"?

CASE 38
Forty-Eight Hours

The general manager of this all-suite property is excited to have had his hotel chosen as the top in its brand. This has led to his promotion to a bigger property, with a $25,000 pay raise. On Wednesday of the general manager's final week, the executive committee invites him for a night on the town. The committee includes the GM's personal assistant, the HR manager, the controller, the director of sales and marketing, the chief engineer, the front office manager, the assistant general manager, and the director of housekeeping. The GM is particularly fond of this group, as they have turned the hotel around from being at the bottom of its competitive set to now being at the top.

The entire group arrives at 10:00 at a popular downtown night-club. The GM is surprised to see many hourly employees already inside the club. This was supposed to be a small group of executives, not a mixture of hourly and managerial staff—the hotel has already had a cake and luncheon with the hourly staff to wish the general manager well. Not to ruin the festive mood, the GM has a drink and begins to mix and mingle with over fifty people he knows well.

As the night wears on, several individuals become intoxicated, and the GM feels that it is time to leave. When he says so and offers to have the hotel pay for taxis so that no one will drive under the influence of alcohol, he is showered with "shots" bought by many of his staff members. He slides through the crowd and makes his exit before things get out of hand. He asks to speak to a manager, and the manager assures him that everyone will be provided rides home. Luckily, one of the executive committee members has negotiated a discounted drink price, so all of the hotel-related patrons are wearing bright orange wristbands.

The GM thanks the bar staff for their assistance and provides a gratuity of $50 to ensure that everyone will get home safely.

Thursday morning the general manager arrives at 9:00 A.M. for the last forty-eight hours of his shift before being transferred. The new general manager will be arriving at 12:00 noon for lunch. Then, she will spend a day with the outgoing general manager to follow him around and get to know where everything is—kind of a quick training session. In addition, Jason, the regional vice president to whom all general managers report, will be flying in around 4:00 this afternoon.

The general manager isn't even through the front door when the concierge chuckles and says, "Hey, Mr. Strickland. I heard last night was *quite* a party." As the GM approaches the front desk, Chevonne, a front desk clerk, smiles and says, "And how are *we* feeling this morning? I hear last night was quite a party." It quickly becomes evident that the entire hotel has heard of the festivities of the prior evening. The general manager rushes to talk to Maribella, his personal assistant and longtime confidant. She swiftly shuts her door and brings Mr. Strickland up to speed on the situation. "Gerald," she says, "I guess we all got a little out of control last night. The bar provided rides in taxis, and four cars were left there. The chief engineer is on his way in the van with the employees to pick up their cars." "That's not so bad," the GM thinks to himself. At least everyone got home safely and had a nice time. After all, it *was* a celebration.

"Wait, there's more," Maribella says with a sad face. She turns to the wall as if very embarrassed. "What? What! What's going on?" Gerald exclaims. "Well, it's not pretty," replies Maribella.

As the rumors went, the director of housekeeping started kissing Tony, an hourly employee who works in her department. The housekeeper, in particular, is one of the GM's favorite employees. She has turned the hotel into a masterpiece. Prior to her arrival, labor hours were excessive, the cleanliness scores were always in the "D" grade range, and morale was at an all-time low. The executive housekeeper, Karen, has performed so well in the past twenty-four months that she has been given three raises and become the lead housekeeping trainer in the company. She is admired, respected, and looked up to by all, from subordinates to superordinates.

Maribella goes on to state that several employees not only saw them kissing, but saw them leaving hand-in-hand and walking to her car where, in front of everyone, they kissed each other passionately and then sped away together—refusing to ride home in a taxi.

Neither of them has yet arrived for work—they are both late, due in at 9:00 A.M. Tony has already been written up two different times in the past thirty days for tardiness. Another write-up would mean termination for him.

The GM shakes his head as Maribella goes to get the two of them some orange juice from the continental breakfast area. He says out loud to himself, "Good gosh! How could this happen? I'm getting promoted, I have a $5,000 bonus in the works, and I only have forty-eight hours left before I'm out of here."

Questions:

1. Should the general manager do anything about this situation, or leave it alone since he has only forty-eight hours left before his transfer?
2. Who is the most at fault in this situation? Why do you feel that way?
3. What procedures or policies could be put into place to prevent such events in the future? Or do you feel that such an event is not determinable in advance?
4. What should be told about both employees to the new general manager just coming on board? Should the exiting GM meet with the employees or leave it to the new GM? Why?
5. In the event that one of the managers or hourly employees tells the regional vice president about the preceding night, what should the regional vice president do with the information?

CASE 39
Don't Park Here

Jean Stanton, a new general manager, arrives at the busy hotel located just one mile from the entrance to a major international airport. During her first two weeks on the job she had realized that parking was at a premium at this location. The ratio of business clients to leisure clients was 80 percent to 20 percent, and several regular business clients had continued to complain about a lack of parking. Executive committee members had voiced their displeasure with Jean's predecessor, saying that he was a "lazy GM who never wanted to nip the parking problem in the bud." Jean, wanting to make a great impression on her guests, employees, and owners, had put her foot down and created a policy that included the following:

- Parking would no longer be free unless it was included as an incentive by the sales and marketing department or as a perk given out by management to a handful of "preferred" guests. Jean felt that the rate of $3.00 per day was reasonable, but, at the same time, would discourage some guests from parking and add open spaces.
- All cars that did not have the proper parking permit in the windshield were to be towed immediately. Prior to towing, however, the front desk staff was to match the license plate to all guests registered in the system, just to be sure that the guest had not forgotten to exhibit his or her parking permit.
- All guests attending conventions, meetings, special events, etc., were to be given parking permits upon arrival, whether or not they were staying overnight at the hotel.

The first thirty days were a complete success. On any given morning, parking was now available. Additionally, the accounting office told Jean that over $11,512 had been earned in just a one-month period. This seemed to be a fantastic new source of revenue. Lastly, and most importantly, only two cars had been towed, and overall guest complaints were at a minimum. In fact, guest comments were quite positive because parking spaces were now regularly available.

Steven Gretson is on his way back home from a sixty-day business trip to four major countries in Europe. As a local attorney, he has left his automobile at Jean's hotel during each and every trip for the past two years. Why bother to pay airport parking? Steven can leave his car at the hotel, take the complimentary shuttle to the airport, and return on the free shuttle upon his return home. Steven has never stayed overnight at the hotel, but has indeed entertained some clients at Saxophone's Bar & Grill, located in the lobby of the hotel. In total, he has probably spent about $350 at this hotel over the past four years.

Upon his return, Steven is in shock to find his car missing from the parking lot. He immediately goes to the front desk and asks for security. Within a short time, it is obvious that Steven's car was towed over one month ago. The towing company is contacted and says that the car was immediately delivered to the county police department, per instructions of the hotel. Steven receives the phone number and phones the county police.

The story now takes an ugly turn. Lieutenant Jellyfinkle tells the shocked Steven that his car was indeed towed thirty-four days ago and, per county policy, it was held for thirty days. On the thirty-first day it was brought to an auction lot and sold within two hours. It was sold as an "unclaimed vehicle" per state law, at a price of $1,000. A new title was issued and no background check for documents was necessary. The automobile's manufacturer, through the Vehicle Identification Number (VIN), had provided copies of the keys to the state for inclusion in the sale. Steven yells a long list of obscenities at the officer and explains that the car is worth $25,000 and is only fourteen months old! At this point, Jean approaches the front desk to introduce herself to Mr. Gretson.

Questions:
1. What would you do if you were Jean? What about the spending level of Mr. Gretson?
2. Who is at fault here? Jean? The hotel's owner? The towing company? Steven? The local police? The hotel's management company? The brand of the hotel?
3. Do you feel that Jean acted in the best manner possible in her decision making? Why or why not?
4. Should the new owner return the vehicle? What role does Mr. Gretson's auto insurance company play in this particular case?

CASE 40
The Confused Consultant

You've graduated from college and have had a successful career in the hospitality business. It is hardly believable that you've been out of school for fifteen years. But, with all your valued experience, many hospitality businesses turn to you for advice.

One day you receive a call around 3:00 P.M., and it's a business colleague you know through the local chamber of commerce. He says to you, "Hey there. I'm having a hard time with service, budget, and other issues at my hotel. I really like your work and I've always been impressed with you. Can you please do a secret shop of my property?"

Two weeks later you spend an evening at his hotel, rating every aspect of the experience from service to cleanliness, from food and beverage to landscaping, from lighting to pool water temperature. After your brief visit, you compile a long list of things you observed. Unfortunately, the list contains forty-five individual comments, and only three of them are positive. It's quite obvious that your business associate needs the feedback.

Since you're leaving for a business trip, you quickly type up your observations and put them in the mail the next morning before leaving for your trip. Just two days into the trip, you receive a call on your cell phone. On the other end is your associate—and he sounds quite upset. He is appalled at your report. He cannot believe that you provided him with such a list of accusations against his staff, a "laundry list" of physical plant faults, and only three items that were even close to complimentary.

In shock, you tell him that he asked for your professional opinion. You tell him that you did not wish to criticize the property, but were playing the role of a "secret shopper" and providing your honest feedback so that he could make improvements. And, in fact, he indeed had called you because he was frustrated with the lack of quality and consistency at the property.

He replies, "Well, I should have known I couldn't trust you to be honest. All you've done is come here and criticize my management ability, my staff's ability, and my property. I don't even want to do business with you again." With that, he hangs up the phone. Very disturbed, you wish you could do something immediately, but you are about to enter a meeting and you're 2,000 miles from home.

Questions:

1. What would you do over the next twenty-four hours regarding this matter?
2. Should you have followed a different procedure? In your opinion, are you at fault for anything?
3. Should you write "secret shopper" reports in a positive manner so you don't upset the owner or general manager who hired you to do the task—no matter what the condition of the property or place of business?
4. What are the goals and objectives of most "secret shopper" reports?
5. Since you're feeling bad about the situation, which two people are you most likely to share this experience with? Why?

CASE 41
Can You Float Me a Loan?

This hotel is part of a major chain. It is also, after a major renovation, one of the chain's very successful locations. The staff is quite happy and they are treated well. It is no surprise that guest scores are also quite high in comparison to other locations in the brand.

The general manager is especially proud of his low turnover rate. In an industry with turnover rates that often exceed 100 percent annually, this property hovers around 40 percent. The front desk, often a critical spot for turnover, is another bright spot at this property. Six of the ten full-time front office staff members have been at the property for over five years—quite an accomplishment in the high-turnover hospitality industry.

Audrey, a full-time front desk agent, has been facing financial problems. A mother of two, she was divorced three months ago. Although she has described her relationship as "ended years ago," the official divorce came this year. Shortly after the divorce, she began dating her immediate supervisor, the front office manager, Gerald. Dating between hotel employees is discouraged, as discussed in the employee handbook. Dating between a supervisor and his or her direct subordinate is prohibited—again, as explained clearly in the employee handbook. Gerald and Audrey have done a good job of hiding their relationship—as a matter of fact, until this particular incident, no one at the property has figured it out. Considering the usual rumor-mill environment of many hotels, the hidden relationship will come as a surprise to those close to the two employees.

The divorce has left Audrey in dire financial straits. It is a true challenge just to make ends meet. She has thought of pursuing a second, part-time job in the evenings, since she mainly works the 7:00 A.M.–3:00 P.M. shift at the hotel. Gerald has discouraged it and said he would help her out financially. As time has gone on, he hasn't fulfilled his financial promise to Audrey, and she desperately needs money to feed her children, pay her bills, and take care of some automobile problems.

In the month of May, the hotel's management company changes its policies on several accounting procedures. One of these new procedures requires each front desk employee to have his or her personal bank audited on a weekly basis. Since Audrey is Gerald's girlfriend, he feels that it is okay to never audit her bank and to just make up the correct numbers each week. This situation proceeds until the date of the incident, July 17.

During the week of July 15–22, Gerald takes a vacation to visit his parents in North Dakota. During his absence, the general manager, Pablo, takes it upon himself to count banks one evening. This is not a part of his regular routine, but he is the manager on duty and figures it will occupy some of his time. On the evening of July 17, the hotel has a very low occupancy of just 27 percent, and there really isn't much else for Pablo to attend to.

While counting banks, he finds that Audrey's bank is missing an even amount of $500. Per hotel policy, he counts banks with Greyson, the F&B manager, so that there are two people present at all times. Greyson, a member of the executive committee, is indeed permitted to count banks, and has done so many times at the hotel. They count it three times to be certain of the loss, as Audrey has never had any such issue before. Confused and upset, Pablo phones Audrey at home. There is no answer and there is no answering machine or voice mail. It is late, so he figures he will wait until 7:00 in the morning to confront her.

At 7:00 A.M., he confronts Audrey as she arrives at work. Pablo, the human resources director, and the controller sit Audrey down to discuss the situation. Audrey immediately appears uncomfortable and upset. She paces and doesn't want to sit still in the seat. As they pull out the forms and adding-machine receipts, Audrey exclaims, "I know what this is all about. That jerk has decided to rat on me." Perplexed, the three managers look at her. Pablo responds with, "Audrey, would you please settle down and explain what is going on here?"

The explanation Audrey gives is that for a period of three months she has taken $500 out of her bank between paychecks so that she can float herself financially. She says that the divorce has left her financially strapped and she just can't make it. She always has paid the money back when she could, but it seems that the situation has become a never-ending cycle. She tells the managers that Gerald is indeed her boyfriend and that they have been dating for the past three months. She admits that she knows this is against company policy, but he has said not to worry, that he will always cover for her. She goes on to state that they have been fighting rather strongly for the past three weeks, and that's why he probably brought the missing money to the general manager's attention. When Pablo explains that he counted the bank himself, Audrey is at a loss for words.

Audrey begins crying hysterically and begging for forgiveness, mentioning that without work she will be forced to a shelter because she has no family members in the area to provide for her or the children. The human resources director calms her down somewhat and asks her to sit in the waiting area while the three managers discuss the situation.

In the particular state where this hotel is located, theft of $500 or more is considered a felony according to state law. Further, hotel policies dictate that if an amount greater than $50 is missing when a bank of any employee is audited, it is grounds for immediate termination.

Audrey looks sadly through the glass window of the human resources office as the three managers determine her fate.

Questions:

1. What is the best course of action for the managers?
2. Who is the responsible party in this situation? Should Audrey be given a concession since she is a single mother with no other forms of income?
3. How does Gerald fit into the situation?
4. What legal actions should the hotel take, if any?
5. In your opinion, what kinds of cash-drawer policies are appropriate for a hotel? Should employees be permitted to borrow money between paychecks if, indeed, they fully pay it back by a specified due date?

CASE 42
The "Sick" Van

It is late August, very hot, with average daily temperatures in the low 90s. This bustling metropolitan hotel has had many crew members from various airlines staying on a daily basis. The director of sales is proud to have negotiated no less than six airline contracts, providing over 100 occupied rooms per night.

As is customary, any available bell staff member can be selected to drive one of the property's ten vans to the airport when it is time for an airline crew to depart. On this particular Sunday afternoon, Chuck is on duty. Chuck responds to the call on his radio informing him that the Soaring Eagle Airlines crew is ready to depart.

With a smile on his face, he politely boards the seven crew members onto the van, turns the air conditioner on full blast, and sets off for the airport. The crew is fairly quiet during the ten-minute drive, and has only basic chitchat with Chuck as he pulls onto the main highway to the airport.

About halfway into the drive, one of the crew members asks for the air-conditioning to be turned higher since it is hot in the back. Chuck points some of the air vents toward that particular guest. Upon arrival at the airport, one of the crew members looks somewhat tired and out of breath. Chuck assumes she is tired.

Late that evening, Lucy, the general manager, receives a phone message from the airport station manager of Soaring Eagle Airlines, asking her to call him first thing in the morning. When Lucy phones the next morning, she learns that that particular crew have all become ill from what seemed to be a chemical smell in the van. The flight was cancelled, another flight crew had to be brought in, and disgruntled airline passengers received a high amount of compensation. As one would imagine, Soaring Eagle's representative is quite upset, and demands an immediate response.

Lucy phones Chuck at home. Chuck answers the phone right away and seems to be in his usual happy mood. When told the story by the general manager, Chuck replies, "I'm sorry. You must have me confused with another driver. There was nothing wrong with my van. I drove it back and forth to the airport and then gave rides to other guests to both the local hospital and Wal-Mart, with no negative feedback."

Confused, Lucy returns the call to Soaring Eagle's local station manager. Instead of apologizing, the station manager proceeds to yell about how he is going to pull the airline's contract from the hotel and how utterly horrible the service has been. He wants an immediate inspection of all vans.

Herself upset, Lucy proceeds to question all fourteen members of the bell staff who worked at any time on the day in question. Additionally, she asks that all vans be brought to the parking area for her personal inspection, one by one. If they are out on a van run, she wants to inspect them at the very first opportunity when they are back.

After several hours of questioning and investigating, the general manager finds nothing, and puts the incident aside.

Five days later, Lucy is frantically paged on the radio. There is an urgent call for her. She rushes back to her office to answer a call from Kenneth, the vice president of crew lodging for Soaring Eagle. The news, by this time, has reached Soaring Eagle's parent office in upstate New York. His first words are, "This is not a personal call, Ms. Manager." Kenneth goes on to say that he wants an immediate report of the investigation, that he feels the hotel has covered up the incident, and that he wants reimbursement of over $5,000 for the compensation that Soaring Eagle had to provide to its own guests.

Lucy assures Kenneth from Soaring Eagle that she has followed *all* company procedures and indeed questioned all of the bell staff who had worked on the day in question, and that she personally inspected each and every van. She quickly faxes him the ten-page report she produced on the incident.

Within an hour, Kenneth phones back saying that it is merely a cover-up. He starts to blame the hotel for bad food, a bad location, small rooms, poor housekeeping, late shuttle service, and bad attitudes of the shuttle drivers. He goes on to state that this horrendous disaster is the final straw and that Lucy will be receiving a certified letter the next business day with their intent to cancel their contract.

The contract indeed has a sixty-day "break" policy written into it. Lucy summons the director of sales and marketing to strategize. Of all six airlines, this one brings in the highest room revenues on an annual basis. Word quickly spreads around the hotel that Soaring Eagle is unhappy.

While Lucy is meeting with the director of sales, Abraham, the chief maintenance man, comes in. He says, "Although we didn't find anything in our inspection process, I did find out that on the day in question, Jeremy had used one of the vans to retrieve chemicals for the pool from a local hardware store." Lucy asks whether any such chemicals could make people ill. Abraham responds, "Yes, ma'am. If you breathe those fumes it would make you physically ill. But, luckily, those chemicals dry up very quickly when exposed to air, so it's highly unlikely."

Questions:
1. What would you do if you were Lucy?
2. Does the possibility of chemicals in the van make a difference? Who is at fault for not bringing this to the attention of Lucy sooner?
3. Is it fair for the client (Soaring Eagle) to break the contract over one particular incident, but to mention several other service issues as the reason along with the one incident?
4. What policies or procedures should the hotel implement to alleviate future incidents of this nature?
5. Should the hotel pay the $5,000 requested of it? Why or why not?

CASE 43
The Prejudiced Housekeeper

A national chain hotel located on the beautiful Gulf Coast has performed exceptionally well in comparison to its nearby neighbors. Thanks to legalized gambling which has come into the county, all hotels are performing better than anyone could have ever expected. With occupancy rates running over 92 percent annually, this eighty-room beachfront property is a "star" in the eyes of its guests, owners, and national franchising company. However, a villain is hidden in the guest rooms, the linen closets, and the laundry room—the villain of prejudice, held by the housekeeping director.

It is summer, and the general manager, Mr. Lee Wilson, has just received his end-of-month STAR report for June. He is astonished to find that his hotel has not only achieved a 152 on the yield index, but that both his occupancy and rate indexes are above 130 as well. He decides to take a walk down to the assistant general manager's office and show her the good news. Cathy, the AGM, is in her office with Betsy, the housekeeping director. They are discussing the day's issues. When Lee shares the great news with them, Cathy says that it is of course her doing since she added such great features to the continental breakfast bar. Betsy, always a stand-up-for-your-rights type of person, exclaims, "Heck, no! It all has to do with the way my ladies clean the rooms. They're spotless from top to bottom, and everyone knows that cleanliness is what attracts people to a hotel!" Lee knows that they are both correct, and congratulates them. Before he leaves the office, Cathy reminds him that she is leaving for her week's vacation to Mexico the following morning and that Betsy will, as usual, fill in as manager on duty during her absence.

On Cathy's first day of vacation, Lee calls often on the radio for Betsy and relies upon her knowledge and skills. Indeed, as they are comanagers, they are both quite busy during this time period. At one point in the day, Betsy says, "For the next half hour or so, it's easier for you just to stop by my office instead of using the radio. If you need me for anything, I'll be in here reviewing housekeeping applications. As a matter of fact, why don't you definitely stop by and we'll look at some of these applications together."

When he enters her office, Betsy is handling a guest lost-and-found issue on the telephone. Betsy is always so professional with guests—she often receives an "outstanding" rating in her annual reviews. As a matter of fact, she has been employed at the property since its opening twelve years ago and has never had a single write-up or day of absence for any reason. It has become a running joke around the property that the only time Betsy would miss a day of work would be for her own funeral. Additionally, the property has remained in the top 10 percent (as measured by guest satisfaction with housekeeping issues) of all similar hotels in the national chain with which they are a franchise.

Betsy hangs up the phone and promises the guest a return call within five minutes. She politely asks Lee to review the applications on her desk while she goes down to the locked cage in the lost-and-found office to look for this particular guest's lost item. While she is away, a horrible situation unfolds before Lee's eyes—but he does not yet realize how awful the situation will become. He reads through a stack of six applications on Betsy's desk and, when turning to get more comfortable in his seat, notices three applications in the wastebasket. As a matter of both national chain and ownership policies, applications are to be held on file for a period of no less than six months, even if the candidate is not qualified for the current opening. At first, he just thinks this is a mistake and that the applications must have fallen into the wastebasket by accident.

Betsy returns with the guest's item in hand and quickly returns the call to the now very happy guest. She promises that the items will be mailed out as soon as she finishes her brief meeting with the general manager. When she hangs up the phone, Lee innocently tells her that he has reviewed the applications on her desk and that he has found three applications in the trash can that must have been there by accident.

Betsy immediately becomes fidgety, seems angered, and turns red in the face. It is obvious that she has become uncomfortable. Lee asks her what is wrong. She becomes very irate and says, "How dare you go through my trash can while I'm working on company time!" Not understanding what has caused this outburst, he says, "Betsy, calm down. What's wrong? I simply said these must have fallen off your desk and that I want to review them with you."

Betsy, now both visibly angry and shaken, replies, "You know darn well why those are in the trash." Honestly, he does not. Betsy goes on to explain to him that all of the applicants in the trash are black. He quickly corrects her and says, "These applicants are African-American." Even more heatedly, she yells, "You know exactly what I mean. They're black and blacks don't clean as well as whites. I refuse to hire them and you can't change me to believe or do otherwise." With that, she storms out of the office, muttering obscenities.

It becomes obvious to Lee, with a few minutes of reflection, that indeed his entire housekeeping staff (laundry attendants, room attendants, and house persons) consists of Caucasian individuals. While he has never considered this odd or strange, it now becomes quite apparent that Betsy probably made these hiring decisions without his input. Since he has been the general manager of this hotel for only three years, he had no idea that an all-Caucasian staff in the housekeeping department has been the norm since the hotel's opening twelve years ago, and that Betsy would have it no other way. As a matter of fact, Betsy has never indicated any signs of being a racist or having an issue with diversity on any previous occasion.

With feelings of rage, frustration, betrayal, and nausea, he rushes out of the office and confronts Betsy. He says, "I want you to meet with me in my office right now!" By this time, Betsy realizes that she has made a grave mistake, not only by throwing away the applications, but also by her hiring practices. After a two-hour conversation, she agrees to attend diversity training, to accept a formal write-up for her behavior, to interview the three candidates who are just as qualified on paper as the other six applicants she has in her files, and, lastly, that she is in the wrong.

As Lee dials the management company's director of human resources to set up an immediate face-to-face meeting with Betsy and schedule her for the very next diversity training session, he still feels quite unsettled over the entire matter. For certain, he believes, someone who just told him a few hours earlier that "blacks don't clean as well as whites" would not be able to be changed through just a reprimand, coach and counsel, or diversity training.

His day had been so great—the STAR report was excellent, his guest satisfaction scores were perfect, his AGM is away on a much-needed vacation, and the hotel is operating beautifully. Now, his day has been shattered. How could he have not noticed in three years that his entire housekeeping department consisted of only Caucasian employees? Maybe he overlooked it because he has Hispanics, African-Americans, and other minorities employed in other areas of the hotel. Maybe he is just a terrible general manager. Maybe he is a racist himself. After all, he is Caucasian and has never noticed the ethnic backgrounds of his housekeeping staff. Will his regional vice president be more irate with him than with Betsy? Will he be fired for his inaction?

With a sinking feeling in the pit of his stomach, he begins to dial the phone number of the corporate office. "Human resources," he mutters as the receptionist answers the phone.

Questions:
1. Who is at fault in this situation? Betsy? Lee? Cathy? The owner? The management company?
2. Has Lee taken the correct course of action thus far? Would you have proceeded in the same manner? If not, what would you have done differently?
3. How do you think the owner will respond? The management company? The national chain? Further, should all of these parties be informed of what has occurred on the property?
4. If you were a minority employee working at the hotel in a different department, would you have noticed that there were no minority employees working in housekeeping? If so, why? If not, why not? Is it quite possible in day-to-day operations that some departments may have more ethnic diversity than others?
5. What are some logical procedures or policies ensuring ethnic and racial diversity in your place of employment? Are these policies and procedures necessary? Why or why not?
6. What about the long-term success the hotel has enjoyed, especially when rated by guest satisfaction with cleanliness—which is a direct result of the housekeeping department's efforts? Can this fact be overlooked?

CASE 44
The Overnight "Vigil"

The setting is a full-service hotel in the southeastern United States. Although located adjacent and highly visible to a major interstate highway, it still has a formidable 50-50 group and convention business mix. The property features 153 guest rooms and suites.

The main ballroom accommodates up to 400 people theater-style or 320 in round-table settings of ten guests per table. The hotel offers a great variety of banquet and catering menus for varying types of clients. The property also has a chef with high local notoriety, and both the on-property restaurant and catering/banquet services have received high acclaim from guests and professional critics alike.

The hotel's pool deck is a fabulous venue for receptions, cocktail gatherings, or leisurely guest relaxation. The airport is just ten miles away. The hotel continues to be the "best in the brand" for customer service. It opened in 1998 and has won "best in the brand" in its region every year since opening, as well as "best in the brand" twice nationally.

The guest rooms are spacious and feature amenities such as Bath & Body Works toiletries, mini-refrigerator, hair dryer, microwave, Serta mattresses, two-line phones, pull-out sleeper sofas, and other higher-level amenities not normally associated with this international brand. As such, guests are usually pleasantly surprised with this specific property. Research has shown that the majority of its property-specific guests rate it considerably higher than what they're normally accustomed to with properties of this international chain.

Justin, a college graduate with a bachelor of science degree in hospitality management, is *very* excited to get his first "real" job at this property. He worked during college on a co-op for 800 hours in Orlando, Florida, in the sales and catering department of a large, full-service convention hotel with over 1,200 rooms. He knew that working in a very large property would offer him the opportunity to learn the catering and banquet department's "ins and outs." This experience gave him both the textbook knowledge and the practical experience necessary to be a highly desirable graduate upon completion of his degree.

The general manager of the hotel met Justin when he was a student. Justin had attended the international chain's sales and marketing meeting which was held in Orlando. The general manager sees a great deal of potential in Justin and grants him the title of director of catering immediately upon his graduation. With a property with only 153 rooms and 5,500 square feet of meeting space, the general manager feels this vibrant, enthusiastic individual can transfer his abilities and knowledge to this newly created position.

The high title matches Justin's relatively high starting salary of $30,000 per year. He also has the opportunity to receive up to a 3 percent commission on all banquet and catering revenues. This bonus compensation could prove to be substantial. The first-year earning potential is in the range of $48,000–$55,000. The hotel already has a seasoned director of sales and marketing who will oversee this emerging catering position. Even though the new hire is titled as "director," he basically operates as a one-man show, with no direct reports. The administrative assistant for the sales, marketing, and catering office reports directly to the director of sales and marketing, although he will assist the director of catering as well.

Justin eagerly approaches his new position and impresses every department head on the property. He regularly types all of his own banquet event orders (BEOs), does all his own client presentations related to catering booking, and surpasses top-end budgeted revenues for both of the first two quarters he works at the property. The general manager feels that he is capable, confident, and not in need of much supervision. Even the regional vice president of the management company is impressed with his abilities.

The outlook is bright. An outstanding chef, a high satisfaction record of previous and current catering clients, a highly booked property with an annual occupancy rate approaching 87 percent, and a fun, energetic team that works together to make success a reality—this recent graduate can do no wrong. At least that's how it appears entering the summer of 2001.

In order to help make higher incremental revenues, the hotel has budgeted $5,000 per month for meeting-room rental revenues. This amount could be earned from one large conference group, or from a series of smaller meetings. Ownership of the hotel never truly cares from where the money comes, as long as the budget is being met.

As any current industry professional knows, meeting-room rental fees are highly contested by clients in today's competitive world. Clients often request a waiver of the fees as a "concession" to give the property their business. Nonetheless, Justin finds it relatively easy to meet his $5,000 monthly budget. His top competitor in town has its budget set at $15,000 per month in meeting-room rental fees. These revenues are three times as difficult to attain, and they have a ballroom half the size of this hotel's!

In late May, Justin is extremely jubilant when a client, Reverend Kingston Johnson, comes to visit the property. The reverend represents the Great and Greater Church of Downtown Anywhere, U.S.A. He requests a beautiful facility to host an overnight vigil for ten to twenty of his church's congregation. And, even better for Justin, he has a budget of $5,000 to pay for meeting-room rental. There will be no food and beverage required, since it is an overnight vigil.

The novice catering director, not realizing that churches rarely have this type of budget for meeting-room rental fees due to budget constraints, feels that "a higher being" has directed this unbelievable meeting-room booking to him. He is so excited after the reverend's departure that he immediately sends a memo out to all the staff, titled: "Catering Director Wins Again—Collects Money on a Ballroom That Would Have Otherwise Just Sat Empty!"

Unknown to Justin, the reverend's church is in bankruptcy, and, furthermore, has been behind on paying bills to all of its creditors for ninety days on average. Justin's excitement level leads him to automatically approve a direct bill application from the reverend without getting approval from the property's controller, assistant general manager, or general manager.

After all, how could he turn this event away? It means $5,000 in meeting-room rental fees—the entire budget for the month of June—with an overnight quiet vigil with attendance of ten or twenty churchgoers. Also, this will occur overnight, so he can still rent out the ballroom for either the day before or the day after the event.

The evening of the event is a busy-as-usual time at the hotel. The hotel is sold out. At 10:00 P.M., the reverend comes in with his wife to set up candles and an altar in the ballroom. As planned, banquet setup staff are there to assist, and they set up the room accordingly.

At 11:32 P.M., the manager on duty (MOD), Melissa, is summoned to the front desk by radio. As she approaches the desk, she sees a caravan of cars pouring into the parking lot, with loud rock music blaring from their speakers. As a matter of fact, the entrance road to the hotel has a line of cars—beeping and honking—as far as the eye can see. It stretches three-quarters of a mile, all the way to the interstate exit! She doesn't understand what is happening. There was no home football game that just let out at the local university. There was no major group check-in scheduled. It is just a hotel full of transient leisure travelers during a busy highway period. There was no meeting space occupied with a conference or group during the day. The restaurant is already closed. The only thing she can remember seeing on the list of today's events is an overnight vigil with ten or twenty in attendance.

The sliding glass doors to the lobby open and throngs of people start pouring in—all yelling, singing, or crying out, "Praise the Lord!" They appear to be in an upbeat, festive mood. One screams, "Thank you, Lord, for this most *beautiful* hotel lobby!" Another shouts, "I'm so glad to be alive and be here tonight."

Shocked, Melissa rushes to find the group's contact person, Reverend Johnson. She finds him in the ballroom, where over fifty people have already gathered. Some have picnic baskets, others have pillows and blankets, and one is even using an electrical outlet to blow up what seems to be a long line of inflatable mattresses.

"What's going on here?" Melissa asks the reverend. "Calm down, my dear lady," he replies. "Our vigil is meant to heal one and all. And you are personally invited!" Before she can get an answer out, a band comes in, asking where to set up in the ballroom.

As one can easily imagine, Melissa's night goes downhill from this point forward. The supposed "vigil" turns out to be an overnight Christian rock music celebration for the church, with attendance expected to exceed 500 people. Many are already in the preconference area.

Melissa attempts to get the reverend to immediately call off the assembly as guests in the rooms above the ballroom start calling the front desk to complain about the noise. There are guest rooms located adjacent to the ballroom as well, just down one of the hotel's corridors. Some of these guests are standing in the hallway, half-asleep, asking what is going on.

No less than thirty-five guest complaints come through the switchboard in the time period between 11:57 P.M. and 12:22 A.M. Between arguing with the reverend and dealing with irate guests who approach her (some even in pajamas), Melissa is at her wit's end. And so are the front desk staff. One storms out without clocking out and says, "Screw this. I'm a student and this is my part-time job. I don't need this crap!"

Melissa asks the remaining front desk clerk to phone Justin at home. Luckily, he is there, and he rushes to the hotel. He and Melissa review the signed contract at 12:28 A.M., only to find out there is nothing in it to limit the number of guests. There is no formal statement regarding noise policies for late-night groups. Additionally, there is no definition of what a "vigil" means in the reverend's terms.

At 12:34 A.M., three cars arrive from the local police department. Guests on the second floor of the hotel above the ballroom have called the police directly, avoiding the front desk, four times in a ten-minute period. Since the calls came from different rooms and with different guests, the law enforcement officers have rushed to the scene. They ask why Melissa, the MOD, has not handled the situation professionally. As a matter of fact, the law enforcement officers at first seem more angry with the hotel's staff than with its noisy guests.

In the end, the "vigil" is dismantled at 1:18 A.M. As attendees stream back out into the parking lot and the band takes its equipment down from the stage, many of the hotel's employees are threatened or yelled at. Melissa is told by one "vigil" guest in no uncertain terms, "You're going to be banished in hell." One of the police officers is told that God will destroy his future life with unending bad luck for disrupting a simple prayer vigil.

The reverend, who by this time has become physically violent with a banquet staff member, is escorted off the property by law enforcement officials and is threatened with arrest for showing resistance to an officer. Melissa can't believe it when she glances outside at one point and sees no less than twelve police cars. And, even worse, the Channel X van is there, with reporters already interviewing "vigil" attendees.

By the morning's light, the hotel has refunded $6,252 in room revenues to disgruntled guests. In addition, seventeen guests who were to occupy rooms left the lobby without ever checking in. Initially, the hotel was to be sold out, but many of these late-arriving guests stormed out. They were obviously tired from driving all day on the way to their ultimate destinations. They wanted a nice, quiet place to sleep. But instead, they entered the lobby to check in and, as one described it, "saw a circus in action."

These seventeen rooms that were never occupied have lost the hotel an additional $3,218. Even worse, Melissa has given away almost $2,000 in free breakfast coupons as additional compensation to unhappy guests scattered about the property.

The general manager, George, awakens from a nice, relaxing night of sleep and opens his front door to get the morning paper, full coffee cup in hand. The second headline of the day reads: "Local Hotel Evicts Peaceful Christian Group While in the Midst of Their Religious Vigil: Manager on Duty Is Called Satan." A large picture of Melissa, with her finger pointing into the face of the reverend, graces the front page. Shocked, the general manager stands in his doorway while his coffee cup falls from his hands and smashes on the ground.

Questions:
1. What policies and procedures should have been in place to avoid such a disaster?
2. What can the general manager do at this point to salvage a public relations nightmare? What about Justin, the catering director? It should be noted that 18 percent of catering/banquet revenues come from local and regional church groups.
3. What actions should Melissa have taken as MOD that may have mitigated the situation? How about George? Should he have been notified? Why or why not?
4. What is your personal opinion of the catering director? Where does his responsibility start and end? Should he be terminated? What problems stemmed directly from his contract preparation and lack of research in this situation?
5. Is it realistic for the hotel to file a lawsuit against the reverend's organization? What about the reverend's organization? Should they file a suit of some type against the lodging facility?

CASE 45
The Disappearing Dodge

The leisure resort has almost 600 rooms and is constantly filled with guests visiting the world-famous attraction located just three miles away. For the past two years, Robert, the general manager, has made considerable progress on guest service, financial profitability, and employee satisfaction.

This particular day, the sky is beautiful with a brilliant sunset on the horizon. Since it is mid-September, the first signs of fall are in the air. As Robert walks the property, he encounters hundreds of guests going about their day. Many have just returned from the mall across the street, others have spent the day at one of the local theme parks, and others relax with a margarita in hand by one of the property's two large pools. Staring at the water and almost in a daydreaming state, Robert is jarred back to reality when his name is called on the radio.

"Front desk to general manager—code 1911," comes a voice across the radio waves. Code 1911 is the code for an emergency; the hotel uses this number so as not to alarm guests with the ubiquitous and commonly understood code of 911. "Please come to the front desk immediately." Robert runs quickly across the pool deck to the front desk area. He is asked by Candace, the front desk attendant, to please meet the assistant general manager and Mr. and Mrs. Hukstentein, who are waiting for him in the back office. Law enforcement has already been phoned. There has been a car theft.

The Hukstenteins are visiting from Shreveport, Louisiana. This is their first visit to the hotel. As many guests often do, the Hukstenteins used the hotel's complimentary shuttle service to visit the nearby attractions. Upon their return, their 2000 Dodge Intrepid had vanished from the parking lot.

According to the law enforcement officers, the 2000 model of the Dodge Intrepid is particularly prone to being stolen by joyriders. As a matter of fact, the police officers say, many individuals have had their ignitions started easily with a variety of household items like hangers, wires, and screwdrivers. While this cannot be construed as factual, exact information by Robert, he assumes that the law enforcement officers must indeed know their jobs, and doesn't question it.

The Hukstentein couple are obviously quite upset and distraught. The hotel's staff brings them some refreshments, and Robert allows them to make phone calls to their automobile insurance carrier from his office. Robert, as many guest-service-oriented general managers would do in a similar situation, offers them a free night and a free dinner at one of the hotel's food and beverage outlets.

A fully detailed incident report is completed and filed per the ownership's standard policies and procedures. This hotel is managed by the national chain that it represents, and it is owned by this same company. In hospitality terms, it is a "corporate-managed hotel" with great visibility within the company.

After the guests check out, Robert phones the director of security for the entire international brand at the company's corporate office. He learns that, indeed, for automobile thefts, the Dodge Intrepid name comes up somewhat frequently for the model year 2000. However, thefts of Intrepids do not seem to have any set pattern compared to other vehicle types.

Less than three days later, yet another 2000 Dodge Intrepid disappears overnight while its owners are in their guest room, asleep. After eating breakfast, packing their items, and checking out, these guests are dismayed to find their new car stolen from the hotel's parking lot. Again, incident reports are filed, apologies are made, and the affected guests phone their automobile insurance carrier.

Over the next ninety days, no less than fourteen Dodge Intrepids, all year 2000, are stolen in the local neighborhood, including from our subject property. The property's executive committee, which consists of all department heads along with the assistant general manager, general manager, and security director, decides to be proactive instead of reactive. They increase the lighting intensity throughout the parking lot. The front desk staff members are instructed to register each and every vehicle type for every guest who uses car transportation to arrive at the hotel. If a guest is driving a Dodge Intrepid, whether owned or rented, they are told of the unfortunate local conditions. They are permitted to park directly in front of the hotel's main entrance where extra illumination (even more than the rest of the parking lot) has been provided. If the guests feel uncomfortable in any way with their upcoming visit, they are allowed to cancel their reservations without penalty and secure lodging at another location.

Additionally, Robert researches the local crime statistics for the prior three-year period to look for trends. Indeed, the hotel is located in a high-crime area for automobile theft, burglaries, and other infractions. He informs his executive staff to train each and every staff member to be alert, look for signs of trespassers, make sure all vehicles for registered guests have an identification flyer indicating that they are indeed registered there, and report any suspicious activity to the security staff immediately. Robert also agrees to allocate additional funding to the security department. Currently, his security budget permits security personnel to be present only from 11:00 P.M. until 7:00 A.M., seven days per week. With additional funding, they can bring on an additional security guard at 5:00 P.M. and have the hours between 5:00 P.M. and 11:00 P.M. covered seven days per week. The manager on duty will be responsible for security from 7:01 A.M. until 4:59 P.M., as is customary policy. The managers on duty always carry radios and are in constant contact with management and hourly staff throughout the property. The regional vice president agrees wholeheartedly with the increase in security standards.

After the tenth vehicle of this type is stolen from the property, Robert really feels at his wit's end. But, when he thinks things can't get worse, they do. The eleventh stolen vehicle proves to be a public relations nightmare. Two young males, both age seventeen, steal a particular guest's vehicle. One of the front desk clerks notices the car peeling out of the parking lot at 2:17 P.M. and immediately notifies security *and* local law enforcement by calling 911. A high-speed chase ensues. The chase weaves its way through the greater metropolitan area for over fifteen minutes. Unfortunately, the driver of the stolen vehicle loses control and the car crashes into an embankment—immediately killing both of the car's occupants.

For two solid days, local television stations cover the story. Each time, the property's front door is shown, along with a shot from inside the lobby. Even worse, the brightly lit street sign of the national chain starts the newscasters' stories. They stand beneath the sign, just off the private property of the hotel, and open their stories with a statement like: "The eleventh vehicle stolen from this local hotel. Property managers say they have taken action. But have they done enough? What do you think?"

The story hits the local newspaper in seven separate articles. It airs on five different television stations no less than twenty-one times. It is even mentioned by a visiting official from the state's tourism promotion office during a televised interview.

Robert is beyond frustration. He is worn out and frazzled from trying to deal with media interviews, writing press releases, and handling guest concerns. The hotel has already received over 115 cancellations within the first forty-eight hours of the news reports. Current guests check out early. Furthermore, the overwhelming attitude of the staff is cautious, almost scared.

As if this weren't enough, the legal counsel of the international chain's corporate office phones Robert. Initially, Robert thinks she is calling to offer advice on corresponding with the media or to assist him during these trying times. Instead, she is calling to let Robert know that he has broken corporate policy with many of the affected guests. In essence, Robert's offering of complimentary rooms, food and beverage, and/or phone calls is an indication of guilt, according to the legal counsel. She asks him to refrain from these actions immediately and informs him that he will have a major discussion with his regional vice president within the next day or two. She berates him and says, "I can't believe you're a general manager with our company and have acted in this manner. You should know better."

Feeling the lowest he has ever felt during his professional career, Robert hangs up the phone and wonders if he should resign now or wait to hear from the regional vice president who is his direct supervisor.

Questions:

1. Did the hotel's management team act properly? Why or why not?
2. Is the hotel liable for the automobile thefts? If so, why? If not, why not?
3. Should the hotel's staff provide compensation or accommodations in the form of food and beverage, lodging, phone use, etc.? Why or why not? Do you agree with the legal counsel's viewpoint? Research laws regarding this issue for your local county or state. How would these laws affect your behavior as a general manager?
4. Did the general manager properly handle this situation from a public relations perspective? Should he have talked to media as he did? What about press releases? Who else might have assisted him with writing these releases?
5. If you were in Robert's shoes, what would you do now? What's your rationale for taking this course of action?